MW00966230

The
12 Simple Steps
of MoneyMinding®

---

*The Foundation for
Expanding Financial Possibilities
in Your Life*

Tracy Piercy, CFP

ISBN 978-0-9780616-5-4

Cover design and book layout by Patricia Wade Design
www.patriciawadedesign.com

Back cover photo by Frances Litman Photography
www.franceslitman.com

Printed in Canada

Dedication

This book is dedicated to the millions of people everywhere
who know deep in their heart that life is not supposed to be restricted
by lack of financial resources...
And, to the professional advisors who would like to help,
but need the resources to go beyond the numbers and technical
strategies taught in conventional financial courses.

Table of Contents

Acknowledgements

As with any worthwhile project, it's never an individual effort. I have so many wonderful people in my life, I am so grateful for everyone. I have just finished watching the classic movie *"It's a Wonderful Life"* where Clarence, the Angel, writes a Christmas note about when you have friends, you will always be wealthy. With that in my heart, I would especially like to thank some special people who have made this book possible:

Sue Ranzinger, for doing so much of everything including keeping me laughing when there is always such a never ending list of things to do; Kerry Brown, for your constant generosity and ongoing coaching and never ending conversations; Gail Watson, for your wisdom, encouragement, and friendship; Jim Jacobson, for making me think, work, and stay focused on the big picture, and of course the simplicity of your wisdom – thank you; Jill Lublin, for the conciseness of your messages and enthusiasm; Patricia Wade, for your flexibility and creativity.

Alexis Murray, thank you for believing in me all these years. Lekha Shah, your wisdom and friendship means so much. Elaine Weidner, Donna Lumley, Tracey Huff, Bryan Bulinckx, Neil Honkanen, Marilyn Little, Jack Shore, Danella Parks, Dave and Lisa Maxwell, Dave and Sara

Mansi, Dave Watson, Richard Larkin you have all contributed in many ways beyond your direct involvement.

All the MoneyMinding participants, members, advisors and supporters, this has been a vision for such a long time and it's your vision, your belief, your support and your stories that make this all possible.

This journey wouldn't be without my wonderful husband, Joe, and daughter Jordyn. Nor would any of it be possible, without the love of my heavenly father.

Thank you everyone.

An Introduction

- Where did you, and do you, get your financial education?

- Do you ever wonder if there is anything more or better you could be doing with your money?

- Are you really doing the best you can with all your resources?

- Does money ever stop you from doing things you'd like to do?

- What would your life look like if money was in infinite supply; if you never had to think about whether there was enough or whether you could or could not do something because of money?

These are all important questions you need to ask yourself.

In the 1920s, Andrew Carnegie commissioned Napoleon Hill to study and write about successful people – people who had found a way to get money working for them, not the other way around. Just in case you aren't familiar with either of these two men, here is a little history lesson: Andrew Carnegie was one of the richest men in the world during the industrial revolution. In business, he is known for steel. In life, many people throughout North America know his name because they have a Carnegie library in their city or town.

Napoleon Hill is the author of *Think and Grow Rich*, the book that was the result of these studies of the successful people Andrew Carnegie wanted written about.

What does this have to do with today?
~ Everything ~

Andrew Carnegie had the book written because *"he believed the formula should be taught in schools and colleges, and expressed the opinion that, if properly taught, it would revolutionize the entire educational system and that the time spent in school could be reduced to less than half."* He goes on to talk about how *"the facts contained in the book, that are well known to almost everyone who knew Mr. Carnegie, would bring a huge fortune in both money and opportunity in the application of the formula."*

Fast forward again: Donald Trump and Robert Kiyosaki, two extremely wealthy and successful business men, have just published a book called *Why We Want You to be Rich*. These men share the view that the money education we are receiving, and have received in our western culture since the 1900s, is not working. The education we are receiving about money today is… well, certainly not at all the type of material you find in *Think and Grow Rich*.

Kiyosaki, Trump, Hill, Carnegie and everyone else who has been able to make money work for them have learned the "facts" beginning with this one…

You will never get money to work for you if you are only looking at the numbers on paper.

In short:

- **You must view wealth as unlimited and you must stop expecting someone else to look after you.**

- **You must figure out what you want and then work to explore all possible options, and then some to make it happen.**

- **You must expand your view of what is possible and turn possibilities into reality.**

How? By learning, by asking questions and by believing that if you desire to live a particular lifestyle that you can make it happen – without sacrifice, without struggle, without cutting back.

No – **not by taking on debt and funding a lifestyle with credit** – by making your income work to support the way you want to live. This important money concept is overlooked, under promoted and narrowly defined: the concept that says, **"Expand your income to meet your desires," while at the same time managing your day-to-day money issues in a positive supportive, empowering way!**

There are so many ways to generate income, why, why, why does our culture insist on teaching that the common, least risky way to generate income is to find someone else to give you a job, give you a paycheck and determine how much income you are worth (and what lifestyle you'll live along with that income)?

Maybe, somewhere along the line, you bought into the idea that if you had an advanced education, you could have a career or work for yourself. But, what about all the other ways there are to earn income?

How often do you hear people talking about earning income? In my experience, it's not a common topic of discussion. In fact, it's more of a taboo subject than sex. It's common to talk about working or about making money (a lump sum of it). Same with dreams and goals: it is more common to hear conversations about work, and maybe goals that are within the context of their current situation. It is not common to hear discussions about life goals; life desires; lifestyle issues that are beyond where people are living today – and it's certainly not common to talk about how much money you're making (or not making).

When are we going to teach our children how to earn an income rather than how to get a job? A job is one way to earn income, but when

they learn how to earn an income, they will learn the skills to help them live their life the way they want – not the way someone else thinks is right for them.

Obviously, someone has figured out how to create income for others when they start and build a business, but not everyone is going to own a corporation. There are a vast number of possibilities for earning income and many more opportunities are generated all the time. You can readily and confidently start taking advantage of income generating opportunities when you:

- learn how to really value your lifestyle desires;
- implement financial savvy;
- implement successful, positive money management;
- and some personal creativity.

At the same time, life isn't about getting out of debt or amassing a large fortune so you can "retire" one day in the future. Life is about living, loving, laughing, sharing and making a difference. Money is the vehicle to help make life happen. When working with money, **you have to make the numbers work, but if that was all there was to it anyone with a calculator or spreadsheet could get rich.** Even when you know the numbers, they won't mean anything unless you know where you're going and what you want to accomplish – and why these things are important to you. It's like a quote I heard somewhere that has stuck with me for years: "If how to's were enough, we'd all be thin, rich and happy." We need the whole picture.

Your life is worth it! Our culture depends on everyone – yes everyone – getting this message. It's not complicated as some might have you believe. It's also not easy. It will require you to change. We have adopted some beliefs that aren't serving us as a culture, but it's possible and it's absolutely necessary and worth it to make the necessary changes.

It's your life. Start today to live it the way you want. Start today to get money working for you, not the other way around. Start today to systematically, strategically and simply live your life the way you want to, with your money supporting those choices!!

Thank you.
Abundant blessings always,

Tracy

P.S., Start Now

MoneyMinding is a simple process based on the 12 steps and strategic processes outlined in this book. These 12 steps and processes are presented here to show you that there are so many things you can do to take control of your money; get your money working in your life; have fun while making as much money as you want; and make a difference – for you and for others.

Within this text, you will find the *Simple Step*, the *Prosperity Principle* and the *Significant Strategy* explained for all 12 of the steps. *Miracle Money Multipliers* are also included for each of these 12 steps, plus a story using real life examples where the concepts were used to make a difference in someone's life. Yes, the stories are all real, but some of the names have been changed. My hope is that the presentation of the tips and stories will help you get the concepts working in your life immediately. If you would like to have a complete MoneyMinding Makeover, you will find more information on the MoneyMinding membership program and courses, exercises, support, tools, templates, questionnaires, ideas, resources and experts to help you on the MoneyMinding website (www.moneyminding.com).

What is MoneyMinding Anyway?

MoneyMinding is the process of implementing, into daily practice, proven universal financial success principles with strategic financial planning processes. The objective is to create individual financial peace and independence because all of your financial decisions and strategies reflect your own unique lifestyle desires. Financial independence means different things to different people. One of the objectives of MoneyMinding is to create a stronger awareness of your life priorities and goals so that you can structure your financial life to support your own personal lifestyle choices and version of financial independence. Ultimately, this is financial freedom – freedom from financial stress – freedom to live your life the way you want to live it.

Regardless of your current economic situation, you start at the beginning and implement ideas from where you are. The *12 Simple Steps of MoneyMinding®* are revolving – you don't do the process once and say you're done – you move forward as your situation changes and are always aware of the foundation of the steps.

The process of MoneyMinding is financial planning and much more! On one hand, it takes the emotion out of financial planning, and on the other hand, it puts the emotion back in. There is no fear, frustration or complicated systems – just simple, easy strategies; integrating the

practical and strategic rules governing financial success with the proven success principles for prosperous living.

MoneyMinding will make the day-to-day handling of your financial affairs simple, more efficient and more inspiring. You will know where you are going, how you are going to get there and have the necessary tools to monitor your progress along the way. The implementation of each of the MoneyMinding steps is a process of gradually breaking old habits and beliefs about money and creating a new awareness of abundance and prosperity in their place. The key is to develop consistency and to move forward one step at a time. As you progress, you will become more confident in your ability to handle your finances, to make financial decisions and to work with professional advisors to get the technical aspects handled effectively and personally.

Imagine how empowered you will feel talking to your accountant, investment and insurance advisor, mortgage broker, real estate agent or banker when you know exactly where you stand financially and what services and information you require from them. On the fun side, imagine the freedom of being able to spend your money on things and causes you desire without the doubting voice in your head filling your mind with guilt or fear. Ultimately, this is the key to developing lifelong financial independence: following through on your ideas, enjoying your money and incorporating the advice of professionals from an informed and knowledgeable perspective rather than one of fear, skepticism or blind faith.

The reward to having your financial affairs in order is having more time to enjoy what is really important in your life: time with your family and friends; time to relax on a sunny day; making a difference in someone else's life. The definition of financial freedom is different for everyone, yet similar, in that with it there is no financial stress or any boundaries created by financial restrictions – just simple, enjoyable, significant living. The road to financial independence where you are financially free and have resources to support your desired lifestyle is a practical, physical, mental, emotional and spiritual journey. Implementing and using the *12 Simple Steps of MoneyMinding* and following the process is the powerful system to help guide you along the way.

Before you go any further...

What are your expectations... For this book? For the MoneyMinding steps? For your own financial future?

Answer the questions below, *before* you begin, and you will be more focused and have a greater likelihood of having the material work for you in your life. It is a widely known fact that when you have written goals, you have a ninety-five percent greater probability of reaching those goals (as anyone who has ever gone grocery shopping without a list knows – particularly anyone who has gone shopping without a list and on an empty stomach). You can choose to answer these questions in your mind or you can put them in writing. Stop now. Grab a paper and pen. Answer the questions. Then use your paper as your bookmark to help you stay focused.

- What are your expectations for this program?
- What would you like to accomplish in this process?
- Why is this important to you?
- What area of your personal finances do you feel needs to be emphasized the most?
- Why do you feel this way?
- Are there any short or long-term consequences in not dealing with this area?
- How do you see your life in one year? Or what are your 1-year goals?
- How do you see your life in five years? Or what are your 5-year goals?

3

- How do you see your life in ten years? Or what are your 10-year goals?

- What area of your life do you feel you need to emphasize the most? (Some examples are health, family, finances, career, personal time, relationships, spiritual, creativity, etc.)

- Why do you feel this way?

- Are there any short or long-term consequences in not dealing with this area?

- In considering life areas, can you rank in order of priority your top 3 primary areas of focus?

_____Career

_____Business

_____Education

_____Health

_____Family

_____Spousal relationship

_____Relationship with children

_____Relationships with parents or other family members

_____Friends and social activities

_____Hobbies and entertainment

_____Spiritual

_____Finances

_____Community or volunteer involvement

_____Home

_____Other _____

- In considering your top priorities, why did you select these ones?

- Why are these important to you?

- What, if any, are the consequences of not focusing on these areas of your life?

- Does this worry you?

You should already see a couple of things: The little word "why" and the connection between the "why feelings" and "does this worry you?" Be aware, right now, that use of the word "why" can be very effective if you use it to ask questions about your feelings. If you use it in a judgmental way, such that you are ridiculing or criticizing people or events, as in, "why did you do that?" This is not at all the same. Using the word "why" as it relates to your feelings and your actions, decisions and goals is extremely powerful. **At the top of your page, where you answered your expectation questions, write in big letters and then circle and underline the word "WHY" as a reminder as you continue to read.**

"Does this worry you?" Maybe, or maybe not – but when you find that it does, you will have made an emotional connection to the concept, to your goal, to your action, decision, etc. As you continue reading and as you move forward from here with your daily financial activities, remember to follow your "why" answer with the "does this worry you" question.

The Problems

It is no mystery that money has become the biggest stress in many people's lives. In fact, I have heard that the number one fear of Americans is not terrorism, it's running out of money. When you consider some staggering numbers, it's pretty easy to see why.

Over five years ago, I heard some statistics in Canada about the state of personal finances that has affected my view of money ever since. Unfortunately, the figures are even worse in the United States, and are getting even worse, not better.

If you are a numbers person, I am apologizing in advance for the round numbers in the illustrations. However, it seems that the averages and round numbers make a pretty profound statement, so bear with me. If you're already thinking, well I'm not average, good!! Except these figures will affect all of us anyway, so you need to understand the implication of them and what you can do about it – either for yourself or others you know. If you really don't like the round numbers and averages, then you have just learned something about yourself, so again: good, because every new awareness is a positive learning opportunity.

The average working person settles into a career somewhere between age 25 and 35 and intends to work for approximately 30 years. When they finish working, they hope to live another 30 years to the age of 85 to 95. Right now, the leaving work event is called retirement. For some

7

strange reason, this event seems to be something everyone plans to do at a particular age – usually between 55 and 65.

Visually, this means our life plan would look like this:

```
            work          retire      die
       |-----------|-----------|
      25-35        55-65        85-95
```

Our average person hopes to fund a retirement that is equal to the same amount of time they spent working. To do this, they start to accumulate money, and therefore, start asking questions like "how much money will it take to be able to retire?" The answer is really quite obvious, yet rarely discussed or promoted.

In order to leave work and retire, you must have enough financial resources to provide the income necessary to pay for the lifestyle you desire. When this happens, you are financially independent. So, our average person is really working to develop *income* to provide financial independence within 30 years. While this might seem obvious, it certainly isn't discussed in these terms.

If our average working household earns $60,000 per year, or about $3,000 per month after tax for 30 years, they will have earned over $1.5 million during their lifetime – assuming they received at least a cost of living increase each year. Not bad, eh? However, if you subscribe to the popular belief that to retire (or to become financially independent) you need to accumulate a large sum of money by saving as much as possible and getting a good return on your investment, then you naturally want to know how much money you need to save?

This line of questioning will produce the following seemingly logical responses:

a) Close to the same amount of money as was earned over your working lifetime ($1.5 million for the average household);

b) Maybe 70% of your pre-retirement earnings because you have been told that retirement expenses will be less than working expenses since everything will be paid for. Hmmm, who considered your personal lifestyle choices in this scenario?

c) Some number that was calculated based on your current savings and income rate using a historical and moderate rate of return; or

d) Any number you randomly pick such as the popular $1 million.

The answer to "how much?" really has nothing to do with an accumulated amount of money.

The answer totally depends on your individual and personal lifestyle choices and what that will cost you on a monthly basis. Or, stated differently: **what amount of income is required to support your desired lifestyle?** Because the reality is that **retirement = financial independence** which may or may not correspond to any particular age, but certainly depends on what income you want to have for the lifestyle you want to live.

You see, financial independence means different things to different people. So, whatever that means to you, you need to start today to figure it out and what it looks like in real dollars and cents. Before you read any further, answer these questions:

1. What is your desired amount of income for your very own personal lifestyle choices?

   For today: $_____ per month.

   In order for you to leave work: $_____ per month.

   If you were truly living your ideal lifestyle: $_____ per month.

2. What does having financial independence mean to you – you personally?

3. Why is this important to you – you personally?

4. What are the consequences of not reaching your own personal financial independence?

5. Does this worry you?

Now back to the problems:

If you estimate the figures for our average family, using this old asset accumulation model of retirement that says you need to save a bunch of money in order to *retire*, then the average household needs somewhere between half and all of what they earned during their lifetime to fund their financial independence – about $750,000 to $1.5 million saved to produce an equivalent of their $3,000 per month income. These figures are commonly forecasted in retirement projections and it's easy to calculate that at various rates of return (say 6, 8, 10 or 12%) on your savings, you would need to be putting aside $500 to $1,000 a month for the 30 years you are planning to work to reach the $750,000 to $1.5 million goal.

With me so far??? I know we're talking numbers, but remember I said averages and round numbers to keep it simple…

Now consider the average take-home income of $3,000 per month and answer these questions:

- How much is a mortgage payment?
- How much is a car?
- How much is food?
- Or children, entertainment, bills, clothes…?

The frightening thing is that **our average household is actually saving somewhere between zero and two percent of their income, and some studies suggest that the real figures are negative;** meaning there is no savings, only debt. A 2% savings rate for our average household would provide approximately $89,000 in savings after 30 years if a consistent 8% return was received on the money, after taxes and inflation. This translates into only $650 per month of *retirement income*. Even with some government or corporate pension income added to the equation, it's probably not what most people intended to work 30 years to create. And, you probably don't want to look at the statistics of government pension obligations. We're looking at how you can become personally financially independent – not dependent on the government, a company or family member.

Interesting how the response to this situation seems to be a growing sentiment among people in their 40s and 50s to work longer. It sounds like they're now surrendering to this reality, or justifying their position by saying they like working and don't ever see themselves stopping. Maybe, but how about having the choice as to whether or not you go to work, rather than because you have to in order to keep food on the table.

Another common response to this lack of savings is to respond with the argument that they will be selling their home and moving to something smaller. Okay, yes, there could be some equity to help facilitate this downsizing. However, is the plan to downsize at the same time as retirement starts? What is the real difference in the price of your current home compared to the sort of smaller home you'd like to live in?

So here's the million-dollar question? Why does everyone immediately think of downsizing their life rather than exploring ways to actually make something happen?

There is the issue of low savings, but on top of this issue the even scarier thought is the staggering statistics on consumer debt. Not including mortgage debt, consumers owe close to $80 billion in credit card debt and line of credit debt – in Canada alone!! In the U.S., it's hundreds of billions of dollars in outstanding consumer debt!!!

Approximately 15% of our average households' pay goes to service this debt!! That's over $400 per month! Using the same analysis as we just

did on savings rates, that means that if the average interest rate charged on this money is 8%, then over 30 years there is $625,950 being paid to debt – yikes!!!!!!!

This means that what we are trying to do and what we have looks something like this:

$750,000 - $1.5m required	Needs $500 - $1000 per month at 8% for 30 years
$60,000 average earnings	$3,000 per month take-home {bills and lifestyle expenses}
$ billions owed = @ $625,000 Per person paid out	@ $420 per month for debt, not including mortgage

The change in view on what it takes to be personally financially independent isn't another cute idea. It is a critical requirement!

What is the answer?? Get people to cut back?? They're already not living the lifestyle they want as evidenced by the outstanding debt. And really, if you look on a larger scale, if you continue to tell consumers who have debt that they are overspending and that they must cut back or they're never going to make it financially, what happens to the economy that depends on consumer spending? We will end up with an economy of penny pinchers who feel lousy and aren't contributing to the growth of the companies they will be investing their sacrificial savings in so they won't be earning returns on their money, which will make them feel even worse, and economically, we'd all end up depressed and broke.

Saving money, cutting back on expenses, getting out of debt alone will not work. This very narrow view will produce one result: more stress.

Yes, it's obvious that being more controlled and aware of spending is part of the solution. The real answer lies in educating yourself on simple ways that you can maintain control, while also being empowered to believe the lifestyle you want to live can become real. With knowledge and new habits come opportunities to find ways to expand your income without giving up your time and energy to work 24 hours a day. There are many, many ways to earn ongoing income besides taking a second or third job; you just have to have the foundation and skills to know where to start looking.

These numbers are very real. Why don't people see this and become more diligent about their financial habits? Why is there not more teaching on how to expand your income to match your lifestyle?

In my experience, I have come to know that one of the primary reasons so many people are stuck is that conventional financial teaching only looks at ways to increase assets and decrease debt – the vertical approach. On top of this, the amount of money that is required to be accumulated in this conventional model is not a relatable, commonly discussed number, and is out of reach for most people. You end up ignoring the distant savings requirement while you enjoy the easily accessible and immediate gratification of the things that can be bought today. Many people will hope for a windfall or expect to be able to play catch up with potentially higher future earnings or inheritances, but this lottery mentality is why many people continue to postpone their future planning.

Currently, someone reaching retirement will be advised to be extra careful with their accumulated savings so they don't lose it because it's all they have. This just promotes financial decisions based on fear of not having enough or of outliving your money. For thirty or more years, you will have focused on saving and getting a good return to increase your assets. At retirement, the plan gets changed to say, "Don't lose it. Spend it – but not too much so you don't run out of money. And, for heavens sake, don't take any risks."

Which number is more common – $1.5 million or $3,000? Of course $3,000 is a number you can relate to and are comfortable with. So here's a plan: What if you considered the income that could be generated from

13

an investment rather than simply what the money would be worth in the future. Or, what if you asked how much income was being given up when you made a purchase rather than simply knowing what the immediate cost of your purchase was? What if, in all your financial transactions and decisions, you simply considered the affect your decision would have on income; either today or in the future?

When you look at your investments and your purchases from this perspective, you can start to see some huge differences: $10,000 invested at 10% will produce $11,000 at the end of the year. Okay, but what does that mean? $11,000 invested at 10% can produce approximately $100 per month of ongoing income. Hmmm... If your goal was to maintain that $3,000 per month income, you would have just handled $100 with that initial $10,000 investment. Therefore, you are now looking for $2,900 more.

It works the same way for purchases: $1,000 spent on something fun or disposable will require one-third of your monthly income to pay for it. How many hours did you have to work to earn that money? If this was a $1,000 monthly expense, it would take over $100,000 invested to pay for it. How long will you have to work to accumulate $100,000?

Saving money and accumulating assets for future income needs is important, and so is getting a good return on that money. Minimizing interest costs on debt and spending appropriately for your situation is also important. These are all too obvious. **Ultimately, it's a source of ongoing income that you need to grow your assets and support your lifestyle. This is how you become financially independent.** Our average household needs to develop an income of $3,000 per month. If this seems obvious, then why isn't this information readily available? Why is it so difficult for people to answer the question of how much income they need to be financially independent?

It's obvious that you need to spend less than you earn, and that in order to live, you need a source of income. It's easier to spend money than it is to save it, and it's simpler to live with what you have than to

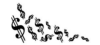

project into the future. This income view of financial independence requires you to **change your focus from asset accumulation and lottery thinking to a focus on decisions that are all income related.** It requires you to focus on developing ongoing income from a variety of sources besides just accumulating savings. It requires you to **expand your income** to meet your lifestyle dreams and to **leverage your time, your resources, your money, your knowledge and everything else you have available to you to make it happen.** It requires you to **change the way you think.**

Please, please stop thinking that you must stop enjoying your latte to be able to get ahead financially. Become aware of how much money you spend on these things and the effect they have on your income, but realize you can become financially independent without cutting back. You can become financially independent at any age – you just need to decide how much money you want coming in to your household to support your very own personal lifestyle choices. **You have to ask HOW,** rather than saying "can't and but…" MoneyMinding is the system to help you make this happen.

The Solutions

The MoneyMinding Simple Revolving Steps to Financial Independence

First, **financial independence and financial freedom defined:** I believe that financial freedom is a state of mind and that you can experience financial freedom; freedom from financial stress, at any economic level and financial situation.

Financial independence, on the other hand, is the situation that occurs when your passive income exceeds your expenses and you are free to choose your work environment. For example, if you have business income, investment income and rental income totaling $5,000 per month and your expenses are only $4,500 per month, you would be financially independent and could decide whether you continued in your current line of work or whether you would prefer to simply take some time off to "stop and smell the roses."

Here's the key: you can actually have financial independence without financial freedom and you can have financial freedom without financial independence. It's all in your state of mind. So here's the thing: **"you need both."** Financial freedom actually comes before financial independence, because you have to learn how to relax and enjoy your money and your financial situation, whatever it currently is. You might be successful in changing your financial picture on the outside, but your

ability to enjoy what you have is true financial freedom, so beginning today you are becoming financially free, the numbers to show that you are financially independent will follow.

The solutions to the financial problems would be simple except for the fact they involve change. That's what the *12 Simple Steps of MoneyMinding* are all about: a systematic, simple, practical, lifestyle approach to helping bring about change in a positive, supportive and practical way. It's about helping you increase your financial knowledge to enable you to make empowered decisions in all your money situations.

You see, everything starts with you. You develop systems to support you and your goals, values, dreams and personality. From there, you look after your family and then build for financial independence. Running through each of these layers of building are the financial and personal factors of your personal vision, personal risk tolerance, the advisors you work with and your tax situation. This means that as you build for financial independence, you will know that these are the important layers within each of the steps.

You will make all your financial decisions considering your preferences, priorities, values, philosophies and goals first. When you operate from there first, the systems you put in place will naturally be personally acceptable and simple for you. The importance of this process is that without it, where your vision is the predominant driver, you will tend to make all your decisions based on emotion, rather than fact. (refer to the diagram on page 22)

The needs of your family and whether your decisions are supporting your goal of financial independence are next. I often hear clients try to explain how their life priority is to increase their business or to decrease their debt. While these things are noble goals, they are forgetting to apply the inner layer first. Start with yourself, and remember that you need to have time and energy for your family. Then you build your financial independence while staying grounded in your life values and priorities.

Throughout the layers of focus, risk is very subjective and can stop you from making the right decisions. You might not have all the facts, or a full understanding of the facts, and something that might seem risky to you because it's new, might be totally boring and comfortable to someone else.

Your vision is obviously the thread that pulls you through each of these layers of discovery.

Then your advisors (the people you listen to along your journey) become important to your success and to your journey, but they are never in complete control. Advisors might be professionals in financial arenas, but they can also be people you associate with who you receive your advice from. They will all impact on your ability to reach your own level of financial independence while experiencing financial freedom, and they will change as your circumstances change.

Taxes, while an important financial planning concept, are never the most important or even a stand-alone concept from which to make money decisions. They are something that is carefully considered with each financial transaction. For example, if you are purchasing a money book such as this one, does this become a tax-deductible expense? Is it a business item? What do you do with the receipt? These decisions all have tax implications.

As you expand from this overall structure to build towards financial independence and freedom, you move into the five major financial planning areas covered in MoneyMinding with the 12 Simple Revolving Steps to Financial Independence:

- Personal Goals and Values

- Cash Flow and Tax Planning

- Risk Management and Estate Planning

- Credit Management

- Asset Management

Within these 12 Financial Independence Steps, you will deal with the following areas within the financial industry:

- An initial personal assessment
- Banking
- Insurance
- Lending
- Investing
- Your dealings with the accounting and legal professionals will be part of all your transactions.

Now here they are: The 12 Steps that will guide, direct and structure your money decisions. They are listed in order, but they are constantly revolving. You do not wait until you have completed Step 1 before going to Step 2 and so on. Your activities at the top of the steps will help pull you forward on the foundational steps (the lower steps), and the development of these foundational steps will push and influence your decisions at the top.

1. **Be grateful for where you are.** Enjoy the moment. The past is gone, the future hasn't arrived. Where you are today is exactly where you are supposed to be.

2. **Know where you are going tomorrow** and what your priorities in life are today.

3. Define exactly **where you are today.**

4. Implement the **systems** necessary to fill the gap between where you are today and where you are headed (banking, record keeping, time to learn, monitor and implement ideas, strategies and systems).

5. Develop **saving and giving habits**. Always take care of these details first.

6. Ensure your **income** will provide for day-to-day expenses including a sufficient savings and giving component.

7. Seek advice and develop relationships with **professional advisors** (bankers, insurance agents, bookkeepers, accountants, investment advisors, financial planners, lawyers).

8. Ensure **adequate insurance** and emergency funds are in place, including up-to-date **wills** and **power of attorney**.

9. Develop wise **credit habits** and pay down existing debt.

10. Invest in assets **to produce income** (real estate, businesses, income stocks).

11. Establish **investments** for long-term growth and financial independence.

12. Diversify with **short-term**, or more **volatile** and **creative** investments.

The MoneyMinding Revolving 12 Steps to Financial Independence

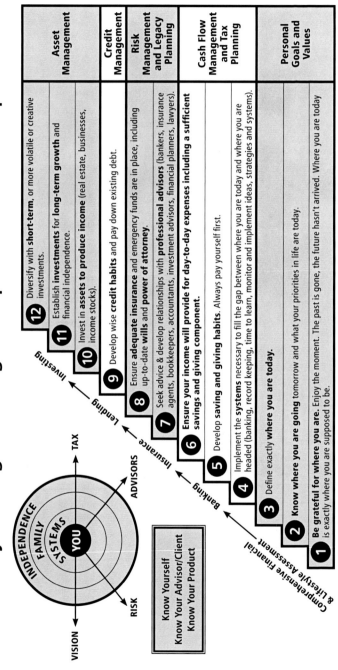

12	Diversify with **short-term**, or more volatile or creative investments.	**Asset Management**
11	Establish **investments** for **long-term growth** and financial independence.	
10	Invest in **assets to produce income** (real estate, businesses, income stocks).	
9	Develop wise **credit habits** and pay down existing debt.	**Credit Management**
8	Ensure **adequate insurance** and emergency funds are in place, including up-to-date **wills** and **power of attorney**.	**Risk Management and Legacy Planning**
7	Seek advice & develop relationships with **professional advisors** (bankers, insurance agents, bookkeepers, accountants, investment advisors, financial planners, lawyers).	
6	Ensure your income will provide for **day-to-day expenses including a sufficient savings and giving component.**	**Cash Flow Management and Tax Planning**
5	Develop **saving and giving habits**. Always pay yourself first.	
4	Implement the **systems** necessary to fill the gap between where you are today and where you are headed (banking, record keeping, time to learn, monitor and implement ideas, strategies and systems).	
3	Define exactly **where you are today.**	
2	**Know where you are going** tomorrow and what your priorities in life are today.	**Personal Goals and Values**
1	**Be grateful for where you are.** Enjoy the moment. The past is gone, the future hasn't arrived. Where you are today is exactly where you are supposed to be.	

Investing

Lending

Insurance

Banking

Comprehensive Financial & Lifestyle Assessment

VISION

TAX

ADVISORS

RISK

INDEPENDENCE
FAMILY
SYSTEMS
YOU

Know Yourself
Know Your Advisor/Client
Know Your Product

The MoneyMinding Financial Independence Decision Making Process

First, a summary of the Simple Revolving Steps:

Step 1: Gratitude

Step 2: Where are you going?

Step 3: Where are you now?

Step 4: Implement systems

Step 5: Develop saving and giving habits

Step 6: INCOME – is it enough?!?

Step 7: Professional advisors

Step 8: Risk, insurance, estate issues covered?

Step 9: Credit wise

Step 10: Income producing assets

Step 11: Growth assets

Step 12: Creative, higher risk investments

Now, the processes of moving through the steps to make financial decisions looks like this: (refer to the diagram on page 28)

1. Everything always starts with you, and then moves from there. Therefore, know yourself first; then know your advisor; and finally, know your product.

2. Always understand that your personal vision is the driver behind the habits and knowledge you will need to develop. Money is the vehicle to produce the necessary income, which will produce assets (or net worth), which will produce more income, which will produce a higher net worth, which will produce more income, etc. when the principles and strategies are correctly implemented.

3. The decision making strategy within each step will follow a process as follows:

   a. Understanding your motivation and expectations

   b. Researching personal goals

   c. Setting and writing goals

   d. Prioritizing goals

   e. Gathering the data

   f. Identifying hidden assets and exploring possibilities

   g. Analyzing the data

   h. Creating a plan

   i. Making some commitments

   j. Implementing the plan

   k. Monitoring the progress

   l. Completing the plan, resetting goals and sharing success

4. For specific evaluation of solutions, the following hierarchy will ensure, as best as possible, that strategies and products are appropriate for you and your desired lifestyle. It is important to know and understand this information and to consider each point in the order listed. Because when you do, it means that if the philosophy of the strategy or product being considered doesn't match your own, as in the case perhaps of investments where you prefer to keep your money local, and the investment is offshore, you would not continue with your analysis:

   a. Understand the philosophy behind the strategy or product and compare that to your own;

   b. What is the type of financial vehicle or instrument being recommended or considered?

   c. What is the quality?

d. What is your exit plan and how do you get out of the strategy or product?

e. How long do you intend to maintain it (what is the term of the strategy or product) and is this appropriate for your lifestyle goals?

f. Where will it be held and who will hold or maintain the product or money?

g. What are the tax implications?

h. What is the expected return or rate of the strategy or product?

i. What, if any, fees are associated with this strategy or product?

If this seems complicated or long, then consider the alternatives and how effective they are:

- **A decision based on emotion:** like that "gotta have it" item that sat in the closet never touched.

- **A decision based on logic alone:** "It makes sense to keep this job 'cause it pays better and has good benefits, even though I have to work evenings and weekends away from my family."

- **A decision based on a partial understanding:** like the economic forecast you heard when deciding what term to take for your mortgage, or the prospectus you were given for your mutual fund investment.

- **A decision based on intuition:** "I've got a really good feeling this stock is really gonna go through the moon."

- **A decision based on numbers only:** "Obviously if this investment is expected to return 20% and everything else is only 12%, I'm gonna take the 20%." But what other considerations are there?

- **A decision based on one strategy or product at a time:** "It's time to make a deposit to my retirement plan. I wonder what the best investment for this money is this year." What about the rest of your investments?

- **A decision made because it's convenient or seems like a good idea at the time:** "Bob is a nice guy, and he said he could cut my tax bill in half – I'll go with him 'cause parking at his office is easy."

This is your life we're talking about. You don't have to remember this all at once. You can refer to it whenever you are making financial decisions, especially for major decisions.

Consider the consequences of one decision at a time without a framework to guide you. This is how, at best, you end up with a filing cabinet full of statements, or at worst, losing your entire life savings to fraud or a bad investment decision. Even somewhere in between isn't good.

What if you only ever stuck your money in low interest rate bank deposits because you worked so hard to earn the money; you sacrificed on some of the things you wanted because you were worried about having enough money in the future; you finally amass a savings amount you think you can live on; and your spouse dies, or you get sick and aren't able to enjoy the money you worked so hard to earn, save and keep? You'd likely feel "ripped off, cheated or depressed."

Is that what you want your life to mean – settling for mediocre and fearing loss of money your whole life? Yes, you can work your whole life and not lose any money, but in the process, you lost your life! It seems to me that perhaps a different view might be necessary!!

Please don't hear that I'm telling you to take uncalculated risks either. I'm simply saying that when you become aware of what you want, and you implement financial savvy and are willing to learn about money concepts and strategies, you will find that sometimes what originally seemed like the low-risk, conservative way to go is really the high-risk way because what you lose in the process is far more valuable than money.

A personal MoneyMinding story: I have lived through this situation in my own life. When we lost our financial resources from an audit turned bankruptcy, I really did think my life was over. It felt to me like we had lost everything. However, when my mother died suddenly four months before my father was due to retire, and my father-in-law was diagnosed with cancer the next month, these were key events that eventually helped me realize that money issues are temporary unless you choose to have them affect your whole life. When compared to other life priorities, money is something you have control over – you can choose how, and on what, to spend your money. You see, my mother had wanted my father to retire from work for a few years, but he felt that they couldn't afford it. While they still did many things together, there was still this "when you retire" theme that dictated their actions.

The big lesson: Don't let money rule your life and don't put your life on hold waiting for money. It is a tool that you can learn to have work for you so that you can live life the way you want – beginning today!

Financial Independence Decision Making Process

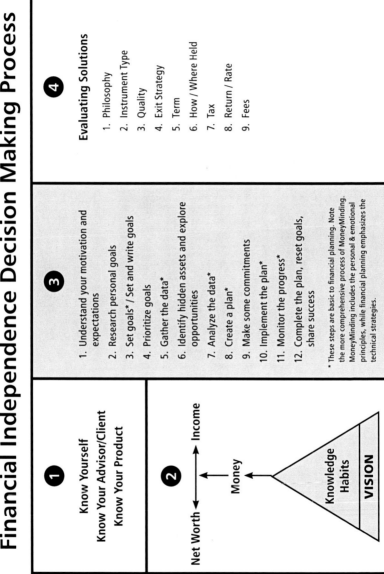

① Know Yourself

Know Your Advisor/Client

Know Your Product

②

Net Worth ↕ ← Money → ↕ Income

Knowledge
Habits
VISION

③

1. Understand your motivation and expectations
2. Research personal goals
3. Set goals* / Set and write goals
4. Prioritize goals
5. Gather the data*
6. Identify hidden assets and explore opportunities
7. Analyze the data*
8. Create a plan*
9. Make some commitments
10. Implement the plan*
11. Monitor the progress*
12. Complete the plan, reset goals, share success

* These steps are basic to financial planning. Note the more comprehensive process of MoneyMinding. MoneyMinding includes the personal & emotional principles, while financial planning emphasizes the technical strategies.

④ Evaluating Solutions

1. Philosophy
2. Instrument Type
3. Quality
4. Exit Strategy
5. Term
6. How / Where Held
7. Tax
8. Return / Rate
9. Fees

Getting Started

The next chapters will briefly explain the *Simple Steps*, the *Prosperity Principles* and the *Significant Strategies* for each step as well as some *Miracle Money Multipliers* and personal stories of how people have used the MoneyMinding steps, strategies, principles and tips to make a huge impact in their lives. This structure is meant to help you immediately implement MoneyMinding into your life for your own benefit.

The stories are called an "I CAN" story, which stands for "Improvement that's Constant and Never-ending." As I mentioned earlier, each story is based on true situations, but the names and some personal details have been changed. If you have a success story to share, please do. Share it with someone you know who needs encouragement, support, inspiration and ideas, and share it with me so we can all continue with "improvement that's constant and never-ending" to support more "I CAN" type rewards for people.

Within the MoneyMinding Makeover program and membership community, there are also specific tools, questionnaires, resources and activities to provide an even more in-depth implementation within each step. It is my sincere desire that you begin today to implement these *Miracle Money Multipliers,* to follow the steps and the processes and to make a plan to continue your financial journey from here. You can receive ongoing free reminders and support and even more tips, strategies and resources from www.moneyminding.com because "I CAN" needs to be "YOU CAN" too.

Simple Step 1: Gratitude

Be grateful for where you are. Enjoy the moment. The past is gone – the future hasn't arrived. Where you are today is exactly where you are supposed to be.

Prosperity Principle:

Be aware that integrating the rules into everyday life is a completely different matter than understanding and knowing what the rules are. Eighty percent of wealth is the psychology and twenty percent is the how to. We all have certain beliefs about money that are the underlying reasons why we are where we are today financially. Before you can expect anything different, you have to be prepared to first understand, and then to change how you think about money matters.

Significant Strategy:

Decide exactly what financial independence means to you. We all have very individual ideas about how much money we would like; what kind of lifestyle we expect to live and the things we would like to have, be and do with our lives.

Miracle Money Multipliers for Step 1:

1. Never say "can't," especially in the context of, "can't afford it." Instead say, "How can I…?" It's never about the money. It's about

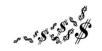

what money can or cannot do for you. Understand why money is an issue in your life either positively or negatively and what is really important beyond the dollars and cents.

Why? It's amazing to me how many times and ways we stop ourselves before we even start. I spoke with someone the other day that was looking for work in her field. She started off saying she couldn't live where she was living because the jobs did not give her enough income. We talked and replaced her "couldn't afford it reality" with "how could she earn the dollars she needed working in her field so she could live where she wanted."

2. Sometimes it's easier to adapt to the uncomfortable situation you know rather than create a new and unknown one. The best way, easiest way, least expensive way, fastest way to learn about anything different, therefore making it less uncomfortable, is to read. Read about how others live, what others are doing, why you might do something, and how to do something different. Reading positive, inspirational, encouraging books will first give you belief, then support, and then the how to. In that order, meaning read books about belief before books on "how to." You can get more from a book than from your immediate peer group because in all likelihood they haven't done what you want to do and could even be resentful or fearful of you moving forward. Read from a positive thinking book at least fifteen minutes a day, and by the end of a year, you will be further ahead than ninety-five percent of the population.

Where to Start? Start with the classics Like Napoleon Hill's *Think and Grow Rich* - originally printed in 1937 and still being printed and read today. It's a book you can read once a year and still get great value from it. Beyond this obvious choice, the booklist at www.moneyminding.com has a "must read" list. There is also a list of books I have read and enjoyed, which is organized into categories for easy topic selection that is suited to your situation.

3. The right, wealthy, abundant attitude required to make financial change, or to move forward towards your financial goals, means taking stock of all that you have today. An inventory of non-financial assets and resources is a critical tool to growth as well as to enjoying the wealth you currently have.

What are non-financial assets and resources? These are things such as your experiences, your education, your knowledge, your friends, others you know, your current position, the place you live and the place you work. Perhaps you have a collection of books like I do. These are not worth much if I was to sell them, but the value in the content of the books is definitely a non-financial asset for me.

A MoneyMinding I CAN Story for Step 1:

Abbey's story: "I am a single woman in my 50s. I have been on my own for over 12 years after a nasty split. I have no children and my elderly mother is still living in extended care with few financial resources. I decided to go back to school after a number of changes in my life including a re-organization in the company I worked for. I wanted to find more satisfaction in my work. After graduating, I realized I needed to understand money more because I was completely responsible for all my financial decisions now. My big AHA moment came almost immediately after starting the MoneyMinding Makeover Program. I realized in step one that I was in complete control – of everything including the way I felt and responded to money issues. I was completely responsible for all my decisions and choices.

At the same time, I also realized I needed my financial advisor to make recommendations on the financial products I needed in my life. I realized I had choices, but that my advisors couldn't make recommendations unless they knew what was important to me and what my situation was. Previously, I was very guarded and skeptical of anyone who talked about money. I didn't want anyone to know what my situation was in case they

tried to rip me off. When I realized how much control I had and how my negative attitude was affecting my financial decisions, I approached my next meeting with the idea that I was in control. That meant that I could choose to share, and I could choose to withhold information, but I was still going to have to make a decision. I figured if I shared more then maybe I would at least get more information back to help me make my decisions more confidently. The whole process was incredibly transforming."

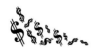

Simple Step 2:
Where Are You Going?

Know where you are going tomorrow and what your priorities in life are today.

Prosperity Principle:

Know what you want, why you want it and have a plan to get there, including a specific plan for allocating all income and earnings. If you don't know where you're going, you'll probably end up somewhere else and someone else will always be in control of your life.

Significant Strategy:

Consider why you desire financial independence and what happens if you don't achieve it? There are some easily identifiable reasons such as security, time with family, fun, etc., but finding the true emotional reason behind realizing success financially will be the catalyst to ensuring that the principles of abundance are implemented easily.

Miracle Money Multipliers for Step 2:

1. Don't let someone else, or society, decide what your financial goals "should be." There is no such thing as "common goals." You must be able to articulate and write your own unique financial goals in your own handwriting, not simply check off a list of possible goals that someone has suggested to you.

Why? This concept has been proven by study after study and we have all experienced it and know it to be true. You might not have recognized the significance of this simple concept to lifestyle financial planning, but... have you ever gone to the grocery store without a list? Have you tried shopping when you were hungry? Have you gone to the store with a couple items in your mind to buy, then gotten home and realized you had forgotten one. I called my husband from inside the store once and asked what else we needed besides salad. When I got home, guess what I had forgotten to buy?

If the simple idea of writing out a shopping list has such vivid results, can you imagine how much more effective you could be if you started with a hand-written list of goals? Now, in reality, it can be quite difficult to put something on paper that you don't have and don't really know how you're ever going to get. That is a key reason why ongoing support and additional resources are so necessary: to provide everything you need to bridge the gap so it's not so fearful, painful or unbelievable.

2. Sometimes a financial goal is simply to maintain your current status or to keep your options open. The rate of return on an investment or a loan is not the most important criteria when evaluating financial solutions. Flexibility is a goal that gets overlooked, yet is essential to provide the freedom to evaluate options, explore ideas, create a plan and find some breathing room, all so you are confident in your money's ability to support your personal lifestyle and goals.

Why? Complacency, boredom, fear or even "busyness" can keep you from looking to the future or from setting goals. However, when you get comfortable where you are, even if it's not really where you want to be, there is this idea that somehow you're doing okay. In that case, a key significant goal has been completely overlooked – maintenance. You might be comfortable where you are, or not know where you want to go with your life, but I guarantee you no one wants to go backwards; no one wants to downsize their lifestyle; no one wants to feel trapped or stuck because they are forced into a situation where they must change because of outside circumstances. Remember, goals don't have to be exotic to be significant. Maintaining the status quo can be a powerful motivator too.

3. Your ideal lifestyle must have a dollar figure attached to it. It's not okay to say, "I want to be rich"; or "I want to be comfortable"; or "I want to own a house"; or "I want to travel," etc. Your ideal lifestyle must have a price tag in a monthly amount. If you want to live in a certain house, how much will it cost to own and maintain? How much will you need to set aside for annual holidays; for someone to clean your house; for you to drive the car you want; to wear the clothes you like to wear; for you to give the money away you want; to do the things you like to do, etc.

How? Start shopping – not to buy – but to do research, to become informed. Go to open houses, visit travel agents, sit in cars, look in stores you wouldn't normally shop in, research charities, go online, talk to people, go places, write notes, keep files and do what any informed buyer would do. If you have an idea that you would like to take a year off with your family and live in a foreign land, then find out the cost. Find out who and how you'll have things looked after at home; where you'll go; where you'll live, and all the prices if you were to do it today. Even if you think you won't live out your vision for five to ten years, you can find out the costs today, then update your figures later, or learn to apply financial math calculations to project likely increases. You need to know the price of your dream, of your desired lifestyle, of your life outside of your current working and income situation; otherwise

you're giving up control and working with "averages" at best. Is your life just average, or is your life unique and personal? This is not a hard step, unless you make it about lack, regret, fear, and self-pity. This is about making it happen. Without this step, even if you won a lottery, you wouldn't know how to use the money. Enjoy this process. It's far easier than living a life of "coulda, shoulda and woulda."

4. Make all financial decisions based on what is important to you, not simply because you want to make more money. Why? What will more money mean? Why are you making that purchase or that investment? What will it mean to you in your life today and in the future?

   Because: If you are not focused on what you truly want, then it's too easy to make decisions that "feel good in the moment," but aren't really supporting your long-term vision. It's too easy to make decisions because you have a sense that you "should" do something; or to make decisions because you feel guilty about what you have or have not done with your money in the past.

5. Substitute the words "financial independence" whenever you see the word "retirement." Retirement is not something you do at a certain age; it is not another life; it is something that happens when you are financially independent and can choose whether or not you go to work each day.

   Why? As you see or hear the word retirement, you will start to consciously make the substitution of words. This will raise your awareness of the issue as well as work towards getting you to rethink what it will take to be able to leave the workforce. Will it really take reaching a certain age; achieving a certain amount of money saved; or will it take the ability to have income sufficient to cover your expenses in the lifestyle you want to live? When you are able to leave work with the income you need, you will

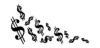

be financially independent. Start planning to be financially independent – not retired.

MoneyMinding I CAN Stories for Step 2:

Barry and Carly's story: "We love to entertain, we love to travel and we love nice things," tells Carly. "Only problem is we are getting tired. We had our family late, so we were able to really enjoy a lot of the finer things in life, having earned a good income all our lives. Yes, we have savings, we have a wonderful home worth a lot of money, but we still have a mortgage." Barry adds, "We love to spend time together as a family and vacations have been a key part of our lifestyle. We really aren't prepared to sacrifice this family time, but we are feeling guilty spending so much money each time we go away. We'd have a wonderful time, but would come back to bills and still have the same mortgage payments to make." "We started looking at ways that we could have our vacations, yet still be financially savvy and not feel guilty about our family adventures," replies Carly.

"Our first thought was recreation property – there is a beautiful lake near our home. We could spend summers swimming and water skiing, and winters doing outside sports or cozying up by a fire in a warm cottage. We got pretty excited about it until we saw the property values and quickly discarded that plan," she adds.

"But, one summer evening, we were invited on a friend's boat – and we were hooked," shares Barry. "We live on an island and are surrounded by water and islands just waiting to be explored. We could buy a boat."

"We can use it all year long, go for short trips in an afternoon, take our friends for an evening or take a week and explore the islands!" adds Carly. "And, when we're ready, we can sell it and still get some value from our vacation fun." "It's a solution that will let us enjoy our family time, without too much financial obligation – which is far better than feeling guilty or cutting back our lifestyle."

Don and Ellie's story: "We are in our 40s with a young family. We are both self-employed and have been very successful with real estate investments. A few months ago, while we were starting a new business and feeling like we should reign in our expenses, we were presented with a commercial property with either development potential or high positive cash flow. My first reaction was total disappointment because I was feeling so cash strapped," says Ellie. "I literally felt like we needed every available dollar just to keep our family going. How would we ever find the $450,000 we needed to take advantage of this opportunity? It was a really sick feeling. I couldn't stop thinking about all the money we were giving up by not moving forward. I had been watching my spending so closely and not wanting to even spend $20 on anything that wasn't absolutely essential – $450,000 just seemed totally impossible."

Don joins in now, "Our focus was all wrong. The answer was right in front of us. We knew the return on the investment would pay off, but we were focused on what we didn't have – the $450,000 or extra cash flow to take on more debt." "But, that was the problem. We only saw what we didn't have rather than what we wanted and what we had – a terrific investment opportunity with a fantastic return on investment," replies Ellie. "That was our answer. We had to stay focused on what we wanted and to keep asking *how*. We had to focus on the goal, not the short-term lack of funds, which is why we now say that "it's easier to find $450,000 than $20."

"And, what's also interesting now is that when we first took the plunge by leaving our corporate jobs, the big concern was not wanting to go backward or lose what we had worked so hard to get. Well, when we look back, our net worth has actually doubled even though we first thought we were broke. We were focused on the lack of money when all the smaller actions we took were really valuable and making a difference – we just needed to see it from a different perspective."

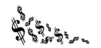

Simple Step 3:
Where Are You Now?

Define exactly where you are today.

Prosperity Principle:

Our priorities in life are not about money. They are about what money can provide such as more quality time with loved ones and the ability to support the causes we believe in. People are always more important than money or things. This needs to be considered with every single financial transaction.

Significant Strategy:

Define where you are today. This step involves identifying in writing your assets, liabilities, income, expenses, spending and saving habits, attitudes and values towards money, role models, etc.

Miracle Money Multipliers for Step 3:

1. To move ahead from where you are today, you will need to learn how, and then do something to get you there. While this might seem obvious, it often stops people before they even get going. As soon as you target a destination, you will create a gap. A gap can be uncomfortable, especially if you don't know how to bridge it. This is also why people often don't set goals in the first place. If

you don't set a goal, you don't have to do anything uncomfortable. When you break the goal down into smaller pieces it becomes more tangible. Therefore, rather than setting a goal to have $1 million invested by the time you're ready to leave work in thirty years, set a goal to save $100 this month. Or, if you want to pay off your mortgage in ten years, start with a goal to call the bank to have them make an extra $100 payment each month. One small step at a time.

Why? Because a one percent change in direction maintained continuously will build on itself and eventually become a much bigger change. If you do something that is easy to implement, you will gain confidence and reinforce the idea that you can make things happen. For example, rather than starting out planning your life's goals and making drastic changes to your spending, how about starting out by committing to keep all the receipts from any purchases made the next day, the next week and the next month. Then, add another step and decide to keep the receipts and record them so you can review them later. Add another step by keeping the receipts, recording them and then organizing them into categories. Another step could be to keep the receipts, record them in their categories and analyze the categories for possible adjustments, future planning, and on and on. It's a process that is constantly evolving.

2. A simple notebook and pen is the best financial planning and tax management tool you can have. With every single purchase or financial transaction, make a note of what you bought and its purpose. For tax purposes, it is far less stressful to take ten seconds at the time of purchase to write on your receipt than it is to try to remember the details when you are preparing your tax information.

When you have questions about terms, strategies and other financial matters, you can record them so you can find someone or someplace to have them answered later. You can also use your notebook to write details about items you have seen while shopping and ideas you have that can be explored for possible income generating possibilities.

3. The idea of putting on paper, either your existing financial situation or your desired future can be fearful; yet, this is the only way you can properly plan. It's not enough to "guestimate" the expenses. You must know exactly what you are spending each month in order to do any future planning as well as to be able to make informed decisions about your current financial situation. The exercise of gathering this information is not to judge the spending; rather it is simply research required to help you become more informed and more in control.

How? Start with gathering the receipts of existing expenses. Then write them down. Then categorize them. Then consider what you'd like to ideally have for each of your categories. Then analyze "the current" versus "the desired" and start to make some decisions – modify the current, postpone some items, explore options to realize the ideal. Take small steps in the direction you want to go, find others who have what you're considering, and keep moving in a forward direction – enjoy today and the process along the way.

A MoneyMinding I CAN Story for Step 3:

Frank and Gail's story: (Author's note: This is one of my favorite stories so I'm going to share it from my perspective).

About a year and a half ago, I had spoken to a group of women in my church on money matters and some of the challenges we face in making financial decisions. Shortly afterwards, Gail asked if I could meet with her and her new husband to help them put some financial plans together. It was a second marriage for them both and they weren't feeling overly

confident with their new financial position. Their big goal was to own their own home within a couple of years. They had both sold their homes, and after mortgages and legal fees were paid, they didn't have much left except some retirement savings. On top of that, Gail had not worked for over a year as she was sick and had extra medical expenses.

My initial review of their finances gave me confidence that they could buy a home any time they wanted, and not have to wait for the few years they thought they needed. However, they themselves needed that confidence. There was no way they would have been comfortable jumping into a mortgage without personal conviction – and they both needed to feel the same way.

I sent them away to work through the MoneyMinding Makeover steps. Within four months, they had bought a house. Now, while this might seem great and wonderful, a house to own in four months, not three years, this is just the beginning of their story.

By now, they had started talking about what sort of home they'd really like; what they wanted their ideal life to be about and what their purpose in all this was. Gail had spent some time overseas doing volunteer work in third world countries and wanted to own something where they could offer a retreat to people who were integrating back into western civilization from these trips. Frank had worked much of his career outside and wanted to own acreage.

So, while they were renovating their new home, they continued to look at properties. They saw what seemed like a beautiful place that would meet their new criteria, but it was well over anything they could manage financially. They both agreed, though, that it was what they would like when they had the money.

A few months later, this same property was reduced by $100,000. Rather than saying to each other that it was still out of their price range, they decided to at least check it out to see if it was all they thought it was. They did, and immediately fell in love. The only problem was, it was still out of their price range and they had just purchased a home in which they were in the midst of renovations.

Did they stop there and say "we can't afford it"? Absolutely not! By following the MoneyMinding 12 steps, and with some coaching, they started asking the questions: "how, who, when, what can they do?" They rallied a group of positive, supportive friends and financial professionals and found a way to make the money work for them.

Within just over a year from the time Gail first met me, they had gone from wanting a plan to buy any house within a few years, to buying and selling one house and living in their dream home. It's a six and one-quarter acre property, ten minutes outside of town, on a panhandled lot and totally surrounded by trees. On the far corner of the property is a rental house that is accessed by a separate driveway and brings in a nice income. Their home is a 4,000 square foot farm house with a huge wrap around porch. They have a three car garage with a two bedroom suite above it for their retreat; a barn for storage and workspace; and the over the top, out of the park so to speak, amazing feature is a spring fed, large clear pond with a clean clay bottom for swimming: their very own swimming hole and soon to be lake (they have plans to make it even bigger!!).

You have to start where you are, be open to looking at dreams beyond where you are today, and at the same time, you must know exactly where you stand financially today and continually surround yourself with people who will cheer you on and encourage you towards your dream.

Simple Step 4: Implement Systems

Implement the systems necessary to fill the gap between where you are today and where you are headed (banking, record keeping, time to learn, monitor and implement ideas, strategies and systems).

Prosperity Principle:

Financial independence is about cash flow (or income) so that you can live the lifestyle you desire and have choices about your work. A high net worth or large accumulation of money means very little if the "assets" require an outside income to support them or is expected to be reduced as you access the funds to support your lifestyle. For example, fancy cars and big homes require an income to maintain. Wealthy people buy assets that produce income that will continue whether or not they are physically there to maintain them. Some examples include: income producing stocks, rental real estate and businesses.

Significant Strategy:

Learn to get your money working for you, not the other way around. If you are required to physically earn each penny, there will be additional risks, limitations on your income and restrictions on your time. Financial vehicles produce results. Learn which ones will help you achieve the results you are looking for in the time you would like.

Miracle Money Multipliers for Step 4:

1. If a situation seems impossible, ask yourself if anyone has ever done anything similar before? If so, find someone or someplace to help you find out how they did it. Often people will say they are too old, too young, too broke, too tired or too busy to do something they really want or need to do. Look harder, if you think you can, you will, if you think you can't, you won't. Maybe there are other ways of accomplishing the task at hand besides the ones you have already tried or heard of. If it's that important, keep asking until you find the answers you need.

   Why? Quite simply, even if a task or situation has never been done before to the best of your knowledge, does that mean you abandon the idea? That's your choice, but history has proven over and over again that human ingenuity and perseverance are key components to creating anything new. If you want something different, find successful people to associate with. They don't necessarily have to have done exactly what you've done before, but they will have had experiences of setting goals and reaching them, which is invaluable support if you are intending to make changes to your financial situation. Creating new associations is like making new friends: you don't have to lose the old friends, you just have to be willing to go places and do things where you are likely to at least hear the conversations of people who are already experiencing the sort of lifestyle you desire.

2. Look for ways to do something, rather than ways not to do something. For example, rather than looking for ways to decrease spending, first look for ways to earn the money. This is more inspiring and will often result in the reduction of spending anyway. Thinking positively and having a "bigger" goal produces a bigger purpose, which will shift your perspective about what and when and how you spend your money.

   How? Rather than looking at the situation and saying, "can't

because," or "if only," or "... but..." keep asking, "Who? What? When? Where? How?" Keep asking and asking. As soon as you say, "can't," you stop looking for answers.

3. If your preferred method of purchase is plastic of any sort (debit or credit card), remember it is easy to spend within your spending comfort zone. If you need to take more control of your day-to-day expenses, or if you're doing any future planning, the first step is to go back to using cash for your purchases. This will help you do mental budgeting for each individual transaction you make.

   How? When you are used to the instant access to money, going back to a cash-only basis is not an easy task. Start with calculating how much cash you need for the day, then the week, or whatever other time frame works for your situation. The positive benefits of using cash when you are doing any kind of financial planning are more control, a better understanding of where the money is going and the additional benefit of feeling more abundant because of the interaction with the real thing. Next time you're at the grocery store, take a moment to look at the purchasing method people are using – the majority will be with some sort of plastic card. When you use cash, you feel more abundant and you get change back that you can allocate for other specific purposes.

4. Always carry cash with you even if you prefer to pay with plastic such as debit or credit. Cash has more control, more abundance and more power than plastic. In your wallet, cash also acts like a money magnet. It seems to attract more money, not burn a hole like some people would think. If you think you spend money faster with cash, it's likely because you didn't start with enough for your needs. If you are worried about losing the cash in your wallet, ask yourself, "what's the worst that could happen?" Then consider the consequences of losing your credit card(s) in comparison to losing just the cash.

How? Start with the biggest denomination you can given your current financial situation. Keep this designated money in your wallet separate from the money you will be spending. As you become more comfortable with this amount and as your financial situation changes, increase the amount of cash you keep – just incase. For example, you might start with $20, increase to $50, then $100, $200, etc.

5. Bank accounts, savings and investments need to have specific functions. For example, an account for holiday spending is best kept separate from savings for a rainy day. Likewise, saving for larger purchases or treats can be done with cash in a nice jar at home, rather than lumped together with the holiday money. A jar of loose change is not as inspiring as a jar of $10 bills that is designated for family holidays.

Why? Money can become like clutter if it's left lying around or tossed in a jar. The smaller amounts of change are still real currency and need to be treated respectfully. You can keep all your smaller change together and have a young person roll it and keep the money. Or, you can dedicate a particular type of coin or bill to be used for a specific purpose – perhaps for something you wouldn't normally spend money on or feel guilty about spending. A great example is the often abused café latte. What if you saved your nickels and dimes for that purpose? It's not hard to imagine handing over $3.50 in change to pay for your coffee treat then sitting back to enjoy guilt free sipping that didn't create a money mess down the road.

6. With practice, you can learn to take some typical financial concepts and see them as positive, rather than negative. For example, we are taught to set aside money for an "emergency" fund implying some sort of disaster could be looming around the corner. Instead, call it an "opportunity" fund and you can see that the same money could be used to take advantage of investment

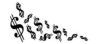

opportunities, "once in a lifetime" experiences or to support you through a rough time financially with more calm. You can also use the "opportunity fund" to take time to find new work if your existing employment ended, or an opportunity to do repairs or renovations to your home if needed.

What other common situations are there like this example? How about "bad debt" replaced with the belief that the benefit of the purchase has already been realized? Is it "risk" or "opportunity"? "Spending" or "investing" in your lifestyle? These might not resonate with your experience, but the idea is to become aware of the way you speak and to think more positively about common financial situations. There is always more than one way to see everything.

7. When you are making investment selections by researching companies, many of the financial statement analysis equations are extremely valuable to do on your own personal financial statements. For example, comparing debt to equity, working capital, net tangible assets per debt outstanding and interest coverage. These ratios are not commonly used to evaluate personal financial statements, but they would certainly give you a clear picture of your financial position while helping you understand the importance of them in the corporate world.

How? Good question! I know that some of this language will be completely foreign to some people, so that's a great place to start. Write down the name of the ratio. Then start asking how you would find out what it means and where you'd find out how to calculate it. Try a financial advisor, an accountant or bookkeeper, the library, Google or a book on understanding and interpreting financial statements from the store (there are also a few in the booklist on the MoneyMinding.com website). When you know the formula, you can start to gather data from your own financial situation. If you think that it would be easier to pull your fingernails out one at a time, then ponder that for a while too.

If you want to make a change in your financial life that is long lasting and is built on a solid foundation of proven success principles and financial planning strategies, you will have to do something beyond looking for the quick fix. If you aren't prepared to take time now to learn some basics, what do you think will change if you receive a windfall? If you are reading this, then you are prepared to learn some simple steps. If you're not ready for this yet, that's okay – it will come and it's a new concept. Build with the simple stuff and learn from these small things so that as your wealth increases and your situation grows, you become more confident and can implement this knowledge and expand its application as it becomes necessary.

A MoneyMinding I CAN Story for Step 4:

Heather's story: "You know, to a lot of people, this might not seem like a big deal. But maybe that's the key thing. I am in my mid 40s and married with one school age child. My husband has usually handled all the financial decisions for our household. We are doing okay. We have a nice home and enjoy lots of time together as a family. Our daughter goes to a wonderful private school and we both do work we love, the way we love to do it. But, I always felt sort of intimidated by this money stuff. It was elusive and complicated, yet boring. I am just not interested in it. Until now. It didn't actually seem like we were doing much. Yes, goals, gathering information about our current situation, reorganizing our banking and starting to be systematic about our spending, saving and giving. But, when I look at where we started and what we've done since, I started to get more involved, more educated and more interested in this money stuff – it really is significant. In fact, in addition to having a rental suite in our home, we have also bought an investment property and are now giving to charitable causes we believe in on a regular basis. And to think that just a year or so ago, I felt like I knew very little about money and wasn't at all interested in anything to do with it."

Simple Step 5:
Develop Saving and Giving Habits

Develop saving and giving habits. Always pay yourself first.

Prosperity Principle:

From all your income, pay yourself first and learn to give as well as to receive. Consistently set aside at least ten percent of all you earn (some for yourself and some for others) – not for tomorrow, next year, a new car or holiday or down-payment on a house, but to turn it into more money that will eventually work for you instead of you always having to work for money. When you give money and other items of value, you receive abundantly from the freedom you create by overcoming feelings of scarcity and lack.

Significant Strategy:

Discover what is stopping you today and explore what has stopped you from reaching your goals in the past. What obstacles, fears or habits have gotten you to where you are today and need to be addressed and overcome in order to achieve success? Make all decisions by considering the bigger picture, rather than simply the individual details of that particular transaction.

Miracle Money Multipliers for Step 5:

1. Developing a budget does not mean adding up the total income you have to work with each month and then allocating funds

within that level. The definition is: "planned expenditures and a program for financing them." Figure out what amount you want to spend each month in order to live the life you desire while maintaining your true priorities, and then look for ways to fund this budget.

Why? You might not know how you'll earn the income that you'd like for your ideal budget when you first make it, but you'll also never find out if you don't start asking. Your option is to continue to scrimp and deny yourself the lifestyle you'd like to live and end up looking back on your life with regret. You might also find that when you make your ideal budget that it isn't really as far off as you had imagined before you put it on paper in black and white.

2. To be able to balance today's financial and life priorities, and needs with solid plans for the future, it sometimes requires some creativity and combination planning. For example, can you put money aside as savings in other ways besides a savings account?

How? Perhaps combining investments with insurance, mortgages, business development or leveraging existing assets are all possibilities. If you're not sure how to do that, then you need to find someone who can help you explore those ideas. Remember, if you go to one mortgage broker or insurance agent and they tell you that what you'd like to do to "can't be done," does that have to mean that it really "can't be done," or can you keep asking? Obviously, it's your choice – different financial advisors have different views, resources and backgrounds that give them other options to work with. This is why we train MoneyMinding® Certified Advisors: to help you see possibilities and find creative solutions.

3. One of the worst financial plans you can have is one that only asks the question, "Is it better to pay down your mortgage or contribute to your retirement fund?" Or stated another way: "Is it better to pay down debt of increase savings?" If you have
or

a home and a government regulated savings plan, you will either be required to pay tax or interest when you want access to the money. At the very least, you need to have some savings or investments that are accessible without any restrictions in addition to your home and your retirement fund.

Because if you are saving for the long-term, you need to think long-term. There are a variety of ways to save for the future – one is inside a government sponsored retirement plan, and others are to establish your own savings programs in such things as real estate (besides your home), non-retirement plan investments, insurance, mortgages or businesses. And, remember, it's not the "big pot of gold" we're working to accumulate; it's the income needed to live life the way we want.

4. Giving money away can be a foreign concept, yet you likely already give gifts, ideas, your time or even used items to others. When you learn to recognize all that you already give, you also feel more abundant and less lack. If you feel you don't have anything to give, you will also be fearful of losing what you have. Start to put a dollar value on all that you give away and look for ways to give. Create a giving fund of cash and a giving box of items. When a charity is looking for support, you will then be able to decide to support their cause based on your alignment to their purpose rather than on whether you have funds to give.

How? Every time there is some income received, a certain amount gets allocated to giving. This process is especially effective if you take this percentage as cash. You don't have to actually give it away as soon as you receive it, but you allocate it for giving. If you run short and need the money, it's a lot harder to put the cash back in the bank than it is to transfer it from another account.

5. Pay yourself first. "Ya, ya. I've heard this a thousand times," you're saying. "But, I have expenses. I have bills. The money comes in and it's already allocated, and then some…"

How do you implement a "pay yourself first" strategy when you've already established your lifestyle without it? You just do, that's how. With a little bit of strategic planning mixed in. As soon as you receive your next amount of money from any source get it deposited into your checking account. Then immediately transfer ten percent of the proceeds to your savings account. This will be an account you set up at the bank for emergencies or opportunities, but not for specific purposes like saving for a vacation.

In the same transaction, withdraw the amount of cash you need for the expenses and giving components of your financial plans. Then leave the rest to pay your bills with, etc. "Ya, but…" I know. You said all the money was already allocated for other expenses. That's okay, because you are going to be keeping good records and balancing your checkbook. You will know exactly how much money you need for your bills and if you get to the end of the month (or pay period) and find you're short, "wow!! Look at how well you've managed your finances. You have some money in your savings account to help you out."

What if you need all the money in your savings account? That's okay. You are keeping good records so you might find that for the first few months you need to transfer 100% of the money from your savings account to your checking account. Eventually, you will find that you might only need to transfer 50% of the money, and one day you will look at the balance in the savings account and you'll be amazed to find that it's a nice sizable amount of money.

How do you pay yourself first? You just do!! And keep doing, and keep doing, and keep doing for always and always!! And, when the savings account starts to look full, you find someone to help you invest the money so it's working for you even harder.

6. Giving is as important as saving. Even if you think you don't have enough money to give, we all have people and causes that are important to us. Allocating an amount of money from every

earned dollar for giving, as well as saving, needs to be established immediately – even if you don't know how it will work with your current cash flow or income situation. You can decide to hold off with the gift or to save the money for a short while – until it's needed (like the end of the month) – but if you wait until you have $100,000 in order to give $10,000, it won't happen. You must set aside $1 from the $10 earned to develop the habit.

When do you start saving and giving? Developing wealthy habits doesn't happen overnight. Start with your children when they earn $10, put aside $1 towards long-term savings and $1 that they use for giving. For yourself, start the next time you earn any money. Transfer ten percent into savings and withdraw ten percent for giving. If you get to the end of the month and you need money for your already established expenses, transfer what you require from savings, and if necessary, deposit the giving money back into your account. After awhile, you will have established the habit of allocating money. You will eventually find that you don't need all the funds you have set aside for your current expenses, and it will indeed be money you have saved and are able to give away.

A MoneyMinding I CAN Story for Step 5:

Ivan and Jessica's story: "You know, I really don't want to have to change anything as it relates to money," Jessica shares. "I like my freedom, even though I have to admit that if the credit card won't accept my purchase it's a bit embarrassing. Ivan is a partner in his own accounting firm and I am an entertainer. I love the freedom our lifestyle gives us, although I have been feeling that maybe we need to be more aware of our money. We like to have fun. We love to spend time with our kids and that means spending money. It was actually with some trepidation that we started on the MoneyMinding program. On one hand I was excited, and on the other, I didn't want to give up anything. What happened is nothing short of amazing. We just sort of went along

and started the process. The next thing I know I'm actually thinking twice about whether I should buy a coffee or not on the way to work. Prior to starting the program, we had been wondering if it made sense to continue our tithing to the church while we were carrying debt – and it was amazing. We continued to give money and we ended up finding money. For the first time ever we got a tax refund – and a large one at that. What seems to have happened is that we didn't want to change, so we just sort of did the activities and ended up becoming more aware of what we were doing and subsequently… opportunities seem to be finding us. I'm going to say that it has been the most transforming thing we've ever done in our relationship to money."

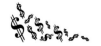

Simple Step 6:
INCOME – Is It Enough?

Ensure your income will provide for day-to-day expenses including a sufficient savings and giving component.

Prosperity Principle:

If you aren't prepared to mange and understand some basic financial matters or set time aside to learn about your own finances, how can you expect someone else to do it for you? When you give up control of your finances, you are also giving up control of your life and the consequences that follow. This doesn't mean that you need to become an expert in accounting or investing, only that you need to commit to understanding the recommendations that are made and the material that is provided by professionals in those areas.

Significant Strategy:

Develop and implement a solid, actionable plan to make success a reality. This will bridge the gap between where you currently are and where you would like to be. This plan will incorporate small changes to be implemented consistently and daily to produce the large results long-term.

Miracle Money Multipliers for Step 6:

    1. Every financial decision – whether to purchase, invest, borrow, insure, earn or to not do these things, needs to be made in

relation to income. If you are going to make an investment, for example, what income will it generate – today or down the road? If you are making a purchase, how much income was required to pay for the item?

Why? Because you don't live on the cash in the account. You need a regular flow of money coming into your home. This amount is a more relatable number as well. The larger accumulated amount of money is not a number we often talk about or think about in day-to-day activities.

2. If you have a lump sum of money that you will be using to supplement your lifestyle, be aware going into that arrangement and plan for the withdrawals. For example, have a set amount of money transferred to a spending account each month, rather than simply accessing the savings money whenever necessary. When you withdraw funds from a savings account, even money you have diligently saved for something specific, it's easy to feel uncomfortable watching your money diminish. This can create feelings of scarcity, fear or lack. The solution is to plan for the withdrawal and to focus on the plan or the reward, not the savings value.

How? If you are funding your lifestyle from a lump sum of money, such as in retirement or a temporary leave of absence from work, you still need to know your monthly expense requirements and manage monthly cash flow like you do with regular income. This means a percentage of the money that you have transferred from your pool of savings is allocated to saving and giving. This way, you maintain some structure and the reduction of capital is part of an overall plan.

3. If you are interested in exploring options to earn money in other ways besides your current employment or career, a great place to start is to really evaluate your interests. Often, we discard the things

we are really interested in because we have preconceived ideas that they won't be able to provide the income we want. For example, why is it that the term "starving artist" is so common? Are all artists starving or broke? Are there some artists who do earn a great living? What are the ways in which an artist can earn money? What are the different ways that an artist earns money from their trade? Can they license their material; create multiple products from their artwork; have someone else create multiple products from their artwork? Can they work as an artist in a corporate environment; as an instructor; as a consultant; or in the field working for a company who supplies their industry? And on and on!!

How do you start to explore alternative ways to create income from your interests and talents? You can do a brainstorming exercise in any industry by starting to ask questions and exploring options. Simply write down any good, stupid, "that will never work," "I've tried that but," idea that pops into your head. If you truly have an interest in anything and have discarded the idea of earning money from that interest, start asking different questions before you immediately eliminate any possibility. Get all the ideas on paper and be open to all possibilities even if they at first seem impossible.

4. If you have an idea for business, but still need to pay your current expenses, there are two types of obstacles: time to work on your business and money. If you had the money to pay your current expenses, then you would have more time to work on your business. There are two ways you can get that money: work longer and harder at your current work to fund your business, or go out and get the money you need for your business idea that also includes the money you need to pay yourself as an employee of your business.

How do you know where to start looking for the extra money needed? Start asking. If you don't know how much money you need, then start asking for help putting a business plan together.

The 12 Simple Steps of MoneyMinding

This will enable you to assess how much money you'll need and how it can be used for your business; as well as plan how to pay back the initial funds. Keep asking until you find answers and the money to allow you to move forward in the manner and time you have available.

5. Learn to ask how people earn their income, particularly when the income is earned outside of showing up for work. While you might not have the talent of a rock star or best selling author, the concept of earning royalties or licensing materials can be applied to many industries, professions and situations. This is the basis of the trillion dollar network marketing industry: a business that pays royalties and commissions for referrals of new business and product sales.

Why? In western society, we are accustomed to talking about our job or maybe our career, but we don't tend to know where to begin a conversation about business or other income sources. People love to talk about their businesses and their winning strategies. There are no dumb questions except the ones that don't get asked.

MoneyMinding I CAN Stories for Step 6:

Laura's story: This is Tracy telling another one of my recent favorite MoneyMinding stories.

Laura has been following the MoneyMinding program for about a year since first hearing me speak at a young women's conference. When she graduated from College, she asked for help with her budgeting.

Laura had participated in the MoneyMinding mentorship programs so I knew she was well on her way to implementing solid, long-term habits and strategies. She told me first that she figured that for her to have her own apartment and to pay her student loans and other bills, she would need about $2,500 per month income. Her difficulty was that entry level work in her industry was only paying about $1,500 per month. She

62

asked me the question so many people ask: "how do I make my lifestyle fit this income?" My response was that "you don't." You have to make your income fit your lifestyle, and Laura was well on her way because she knew how she wanted to live and had implemented systems to save, give and maintain solid financial management strategies.

During our discussion, she mentioned casually how it would have been so much easier if she had just been hired for a job she had recently applied for. I asked her about it and it turns out to be a job in her industry paying $70,000 per year, or about $3,500 per month (after taxes). Well, this changed everything. We discussed the position and how she felt qualified to apply because it was the sort of work she had done during the summer months. When she was turned down, she was told she needed more experience. So, Laura did what many people would do: settle in to get some experience and work her way up the ranks to eventually qualify for the $70,000 job – which she already felt she could do.

We analyzed the $70,000 and figured that it really represented about $40 an hour of full-time wages on a contract basis. Laura thought this was a reasonable wage for a contractor in her industry so we sent her off to interview people in contract positions to ask them how they got their work, what they did, who paid them, how much they charged, etc.

Three months later, I received a message from Laura informing me of her new company name. She had registered a company and printed some business cards. In the fourth month, she told me she was moving away for a while so we arranged to meet before she left. She had secured a contract in a northern community for her new company to do all the work she went to school for and would have been doing for the $70,000 per year job. Because she was very mobile and keen to work at what she trained to do, she was off right away. Her contract was worth $95,000 per year!!! Not bad for someone who was trying to figure out how to live on an entry-level wage of $1,500 per month ($18,000 per year) four months before.

Allison's story: "I have been pretty unhappy in my job for a while. I'm in my late 40s and I like the industry I work in, but am on my own and it seems that the only way to really move ahead with my career would be to leave my job and take a commissioned sales position. I don't want to do that at this point in my life. I have worked for commission before and have been through a lot of changes in my life and didn't feel that it was the right time to go back to that uncertain income. I started doing some serious looking at my goals and life interests and discovered a wonderful product that was available through a network marketing company. After exploring the business further, I decided this was my answer. It was fun; not at all technical or stressful like my career work; and I could work at it part-time while I was still working full-time. Now I'm doing work I love; I'm excited, happy; and making extra income and it all seems to make my regular job easier to handle."

Kathy's story: "I had a corporate job which ended suddenly a year or so ago. I had been sort of thinking that I needed a change because the travel was starting to wear me down so the change was in some ways welcome. I had already begun looking at my financial and personal goals, but hadn't put any sort of plan in place yet. I did have some savings so when the job ended I could afford the time to figure out my next step. Well, except that I was offered another position very quickly. I took it, but really wanted to start to create something for myself.

My new role was relatively easy compared to the last one and has given me the time I wanted to think and plan. One of my personal goals was to clean up and sort through years of stuff that I'd accumulated in anticipation of moving to a new home sometime soon. While I was puttering away, I created notes and cards to keep me on track and focused. Each week, I would simply write down the organizing, de-cluttering areas for tackling that week and I'd stick to it without getting sidetracked or overwhelmed.

That's when it hit me. This was fun. It was simple. I bet other people could benefit from a simple little system like this. I didn't want to make a career of it, but I got excited about the idea of creating a product that Organizers and others could use to help people cull through their stuff like I was doing. So… I created some proto-types, found a graphic artist, got the necessary copyright information, registered a business name, and am just finishing up my marketing and business plan – all while puttering about with my own stuff and continuing to work full-time."

Simple Step 7:
Professional Advisors

Seek advice and develop relationships with professional advisors (bankers, insurance agents, bookkeepers, accountants, investment advisors, financial planners, lawyers).

Prosperity Principle:

Clutter will distract you from achieving financial goals. The little pieces of paper – unpaid bills, post-it notes, junk drawers, jammed closets and filing areas – keep you from focusing on the really important areas of your life and leave little room for new opportunities or projects that could help financially. Why is it that you are holding on to that "it could come in handy one day" object or that "just in case" item you might need at a later time? This scarcity thinking will prevent you from realizing true abundance.

Significant Strategy:

Find the time and space to think and work by getting organized, cleaning any clutter and giving away anything that does not serve you now or in the life you expect to live. When you hold on to something that you are not currently using or enjoying, "just in case" you might need it, you are preventing yourself from moving forward. Too much "stuff" becomes clutter and doesn't leave any room for growth or change.

Miracle Money Multipliers for Step 7:

1. For every single financial transaction, write in your own words your expectations and understanding of the product, strategy or investment. This simple letter of understanding will assist you in communicating with the advisor who is helping you with the transaction; it will help you remember details later on; and it will help anyone who might need to help you with your financial matters if you weren't able to. If you can have the advisor sign the document as well, even better, but understand this is not a legal document; it is for clarity of communication and understanding only.

   Why take the time when a letter of understanding isn't a legal document? First, by writing out your letter of understanding, you will ensure that you and your advisor are on the same page as far as communicating your needs and the product's ability to fulfill that need. Second, for future reference, your reasons and details are not as clear after several years have passed as they are when you first purchase the financial product. The letter of understanding is a great summary of your expectations at the time of purchase. Third, if someone else is required to handle your financial affairs, they will understand what you have and why. For estate purposes, or for medical reasons, a letter of understanding can be an invaluable tool – to be kept with your record of affairs – that your executor, power of attorney or next of kin will use to process your estate.

2. Something that will hold you back and can create unexpected risk is excess clutter in your life. This clutter can be stuff, paper, activities or even people. It's anything that blocks the calm space you need to address changing financial issues. You must have the time, energy and space to work, learn, manage and grow. If this is your situation, you first need to acknowledge the obstacle and risks it creates, and then handle one decision at a time until you have the surroundings that support you in your financial growth.

If this doesn't seem significant, ask yourself whether the clutter, the negative people or the activities exist in your vision of your ideal life. And, what is the cost of the clutter? What will it cost you if you lose an important financial paper during a tax audit, for example? Likely, your ideal lifestyle is not cluttered with papers, stuff and negative people; therefore, this requires clearing up before you can move ahead.

How? Start with a list of all the areas where clutter is bothering you, and then list all of the clutter items. After you have a list, start to prioritize rooms, areas and sections in your home and your life. Then, make a plan, set some dates, book some time and follow through.

3. Staying in control of your investments and your financial planning does not require you to become an expert on all the technical aspects; it requires you to know what your responsibilities are and how you will fulfill them. For example, if you are investing in stocks, bonds or mutual funds, you will be in more control if you have read the investor material presented to you, written your letter of understanding, know your exit plan and know how, where and what to look for when monitoring the investments.

   Why? Even the most knowledgeable advisors with the most experience are still not living your life. You are ultimately responsible for each financial decision you make. Learn what your responsibilities are, what you need to know and what you require to stay in control of your finances from experienced advisors.

4. Understanding the technical aspects of financial planning, financial products, financial markets, economic indicators and taxes – while part of financial literacy – is not where you start your financial education. If you are not interested in financial matters, or do not take the time to learn them, it doesn't mean that you can't be in control and realize financial success.

What do you need to know? What do you have? When does it need your attention? How are you going to monitor it? Why do you have it? Where will you monitor it? When and how will you get rid of it? These are questions to ask yourself that will be more valuable than trying to cram the technical knowledge of your advisor into a short education on the product.

5. Many of the skills required to build and manage an investment portfolio are extensions of skills that are learned through sound personal money management. For example, balancing a checkbook requires an analysis of the transactions and a comparison of a bank produced statement. Evaluating corporate financial statements involves an analysis of the transactions and comparisons to other statements, industry standards or to different types of statements. Yes, evaluating corporate financial statements is much more involved, but both require similar skills. Learn to see the big picture. If you can handle the small stuff, your financial growth will evolve naturally.

How? Start documenting financial transactions on paper, and then progress to an electronic money program. Start with simple tracking, then balancing, crosschecking and analyzing. If you compare the process to learning math in school, you learn multiplication and division longhand before graduating to a calculator. And, you learn the calculator before moving on to a spreadsheet. It's the same process. Start with your personal financial statements, then towards corporate financial statements for investment purposes, and then for your own business or private company. Your investments will evolve as your skill level and comfort with the process expands.

MoneyMinding I CAN Stories for Step 7:

Paul and Rachael's story: This is another story that needs to be partially told from my perspective: Paul and Rachael first contacted

MoneyMinding after reading an article I had written on "Grandma's Lessons on Financial Management." They are both in their 40s and have one young daughter in school. Their initial goals were to get organized financially so they could have some sort of overall plan. Prior to MoneyMinding, they had a seemingly large number of statements for credit cards, lines of credit, investments, insurances and loans. They were concerned about making ends meet and, at one point, were contemplating selling their home and downsizing to pay off everything, consolidate and simplify their finances to essentially start again.

"We both loved our home and our neighborhood and had been excited for the day when we could live in the house without a tenant in the suite," comments Rachael. "But, for some reason, everything seemed to be so complicated and overwhelming with our finances that we just didn't know where to start or where to turn to sort things out. It seemed that the easiest way was to just start over," says Paul. "We really did have to go right back to the basics and start over, but not by selling everything and downsizing," adds Rachael.

Their situation was really quite simple when you use the steps. They had become so overwhelmed with the paperwork and details of the various pieces that had become their financial plan by default that they really couldn't see past the numbers. There really wasn't a major crisis to handle; it just seemed like it because there were so many small pieces. Paul and Rachael began working on their goals first. They then used cash for purchases and started tracking all their expenses. At the same time, all the details of their existing finances were slowly gathered into proper personal financial statements so they and their advisors could see exactly what they had in place. Some tracking and organizing systems were put in place and, best of all, they got really connected to some goals that had previously seemed to be slipping away with their old finances: take back their whole house (i.e. have no suite or tenant anymore), take a year to live in France when their daughter was in the fifth grade, and get a dog. All this enabled them to pull together a real financial plan that included savings and investing, debt reduction, risk management and overall cash management.

What I love so much about Paul and Rachel's story is that they are actually doing exactly what they set out to do. It has taken them just over two years, but they have completely changed their whole attitude towards money, the way they handle it and how they approach money decisions. In fact, just before their tenant moved out, they were having second thoughts and feeling insecure about their plans. A realtor they met listened as they re-told of their previous plans to downsize their home to free up more cash. Gratefully, Rachel told me of the realtor's insistence that it was in their best interest to sell their big home first, then find something to move into that was smaller because then they would know exactly how much money they'd have to purchase the new home with.

To say that I flipped, might be a bit of an understatement. They were doing so well towards their goals and with their plans, and in a moment of insecurity, they almost fell victim to a plan that was surely not in their best interest. If it really did make sense for them to move (which it did not), it would have been simple math to calculate the equity in their home that could have been used for a new home with much less stress and simplicity.

"I guess we just needed to be encouraged and re-told that our dream to live in France could be a reality and that our plan really would work if we were patient with it," comments Rachael. "I'm not really sure what we were feeling at the time – certainly not confident about our future and our ability to reach our goals." "It's interesting now to look back at that time because we really are going to make it all happen and then some," boasts Paul. "We are living in our whole house with no tenant, we have an awesome dog and we're leaving for France for six months this coming July. And, on top of that, the dog breeder will take the dog for the time we're away. We intentionally changed the plan from one year to six months so we haven't compromised on the plans that way. The part we hadn't anticipated is that we're even considering buying a second property

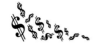

using some of our home's equity rather than downsizing. We just haven't found the right place yet, and aren't totally sure if we want to buy now or wait until we return from France. Either way, we are definitely looking at expanding our finances rather than cutting back and starting over."

Karen's story: "I am a Certified Financial Planner (CFP) who has been in the financial industry for over 30 years. I have seen more interesting and creative ways of trying to make financial situations work from people putting pieces of information together from only partial understanding. Some things people have tried to do to save a few thousand dollars in taxes on an estate are just so sad. These people think they are doing the right thing, but are afraid to ask or don't know how to ask and end up creating huge messes down the road.

With investments, many people leave slow, but steady investments to go chasing after some high returning something or other that their friend at work has recommended. It's not that they have to stay in low returning investments; it's that they have to be able to make the investment decisions with the right foundation beneath them, and with the right amount of money so they won't end up losing their life savings. Chasing a high return is never the right choice. But this doesn't mean it's not important, it just means there has to be a strategy, some knowledge and some systems in place to make the selections for higher returning investment choices. Unfortunately, in the industry, we aren't taught how to help people through the emotional ups and downs of these sorts of decisions. It's very difficult because you want to help, but people are just constantly focused on saving a few bucks or making a windfall and they won't listen to reason – the emotion of the pay off is always stronger than the risks.

I have finally come to realize that the logical answer will come when someone can emotionally relate to the benefits as well as the consequences. It also helps when they understand why they are doing something and why they aren't doing other things. When they understand their motivation, it also helps them articulate what

they know and don't know about their financial transactions. People will make the right decisions when they have the right foundation of technical and emotional skills."

Simple Step 8:
Risk, Insurance, Estate Issues
Covered?

Ensure adequate insurance and emergency funds are in place including an up-to-date will and power of attorney.

Prosperity Principle:

The only true way to reduce financial risk is to diversify your income and investments and be open to receiving new ideas and opportunities. Understand that you will lose money at some point so be prepared and know what the risks are ahead of time. Wealthy people also know that when giving and receiving work together, you don't get one without the other. In this way, your money is working for you and not the other way around.

Significant Strategy:

Calculate your current risk exposure and be clear on the potential risk of doing something as well as the potential risk of not doing something. There are risks in everything you do. Learn to become aware of your exposure to risk and stay comfortable with it.

Miracle Money Multipliers for Step 8:

1. Life insurance is not just for your survivors when you die. It can be a phenomenal planning tool with great benefits for you while

you're alive. To benefit, however, you will need to plan ahead and be open to seeing beyond the premium payments and the death benefit and see the opportunities that insurance can provide you today: peace of mind and benefits for you if you don't die, but aren't able to carry on your normal duties, to name just two.

Why should you really add an additional expense to insure something that might not happen? One, often overlooked benefit, is simply the peace of mind you get taking the steps needed to move you forward in your financial planning. If you know you are protected, should things get really bad or some unexpected situation arises, you have more confidence when investing, starting a business, changing your income source and enjoying your life.

2. Just because an investment or financial product is okay for your friend, family or advisor does not mean it is okay for you. If you know of an investment that is working well for someone and you are considering it for yourself, remember that they have already had a head start – you don't know the details of that person's financial situation. We all have different goals, experience, values and frames of reference from which we make investment and financial decisions. Likewise, just because something didn't work for your friend or relative, does not mean that it won't work for you.

    Why? You must make all your decisions in the context of your own personal goals, vision, desires, values and knowledge. Every financial transaction starts with knowing yourself: your motivation; your values; your priorities; your key influences; your past experience; your goals; and what you expect – and why – from the transaction.

3. When your security of income depends on someone else to provide it for you, such as when you have a job or government benefits, you are also at the mercy or that person, employer, government or institution if they decide to change the amount

or the way they pay you. If someone is providing you with your income, they can also provide you with your layoff notice.

What do you do if you only have one source of income? Start by recognizing the additional risk your household is exposed to; then work to protect yourself with insurance, savings, income-producing investments, a home business or royalties.

4. Within a household, you need to have multiple sources of income, as well as multiple assets, to build true financial security. If both income earners work for the same company, or in the same industry, there is very little security in that.

How can you minimize this risk? Like investing, where one risk minimization strategy is to diversify among industries, type of investment or return, the same is true for income within a family. For planning purposes, it's best to have income into your home from different industries, types of income (such as employment, self-employed, business or investment), payment frequency, etc. This way, you cover your risk of income loss. Ideally, you will want to ensure you have income that will continue regardless of whether you work to receive it, for example, investment income, royalty income, disability insurance, etc.

A MoneyMinding I CAN Story for Step 8:

Oriana's story: "I am turning 60 this year. I would love to own my own condo. I was working hard to save enough money so I could buy a place and also have enough put aside so I would have cash available in case something happened to me like it did a few years ago when I had my car accident and couldn't work. I had to sell almost everything I owned just to keep paying the bills. It was horrible. I'm not going to let that happen when I've bought real estate!!"

"What is so cool, now, is that I realized through the MoneyMinding steps that there are ways to cover that risk. I had first thought that

everything needed to get saved so I could accumulate the money I needed for the condo, for my emergency fund and for my retirement. Now, I have bought insurance to protect my income and I'm building my business to provide ongoing revenue from product sales and licensing instead of working for an hourly consulting fee. Even my training seminars are now structured differently so there is more ongoing income from each activity I do. Because I have the insurance, I have the peace of mind to focus on my business rather than worrying that everything might come crumbling down. It was amazing, really, how that shift in perspective from building savings to protecting my income and creating ongoing income has made all the difference in my life. Now, I'm even exploring business funding rather than trying to build my business with my line of credit and my credit card. I have learned how to calculate the return on investment so I can see the benefit to raising money rather than scrimping, saving and waiting to expand my business. It is all connected and has been a logical progression at each step."

Mark and Nora's story: "We are both just 50. Our kids are older and all going to university and starting careers. I had always wanted to live on the coast," remarks Nora. "Mark agreed, but didn't know if it made sense financially." "Where we lived, we had a big beautiful home, a successful retail store and we were well established. Homes on the coast are much more expensive and we really didn't know what we would do for work when we got here," he adds.

"We would have to sell the business; find a home large enough for our family; then figure out what to do for income," Nora shares emotionally. "Most of our advisors thought we were crazy. They looked at our savings, and what we could get for the business and our home and said it didn't make sense financially. "They were right, I guess. Except, that we knew that if we didn't go now, it would likely not happen; our kids would go off to university across the country and settle somewhere to have their families and we would end up staying put in our comfortable (but uncomfortable) way so they could have their home to come back to. I felt that if we went now, as they were finishing school, they would find a new home in our new city on the coast. We were experienced in a lot of retail and marketing business ventures and could make our own work while we still have the energy and drive." Mark adds, "While it was a frightening thought, the excitement of starting over was stronger."

"We got focused on our goal, kept our family priorities in line, and worked with our advisors to make the move financially viable," he comments. "Now we are both doing contract work at meaningful and exciting work. Our kids are involved in our life and their own, and we have found a beautiful home for all of us, including the dog. We networked with other professionals in the new city, got acquainted with the business environment here and have established relationships with key advisors who support our dreams here now too," smiles Nora. "I'm just so grateful we found some supportive people and didn't just listen to the nah-sayers who said it was risky. With their support, we had a plan and calculated our risks, and the rewards are wonderful – and our kids get to see us following our dream – that's a nice extra bonus we hadn't thought of."

Simple Step 9: Credit Wise

Develop wise credit habits and pay down existing debt.

Prosperity Principle:

What are you doing in your life that can be leveraged? Do you currently have tasks that can be done by someone else freeing up your time so that you're more productive and can enjoy your life more? Time is your most valuable asset and it is the one thing that cannot be replaced once spent. Use your time wisely and don't be afraid to delegate and/or pay someone else to do some of your tasks.

Significant Strategy:

Manage your time and priorities. This will involve analyzing all your current activities and deciding what will serve you best on your journey to financial independence. This will also help you to stay focused on the result and not get sidetracked by short-term obstacles or unproductive activities.

Miracle Money Multipliers for Step 9:

1. It is important to realize that even if you pay off your credit card balance monthly, you are really always one month in arrears with your payments. A better spending habit is to gradually adjust your spending so it is in real time, meaning that you pay as you go – or have some expenses prepaid on your credit card.

Why? If your credit card is paid in advance or expenses are paid in real time, you will have at least one month of expenses set aside if you weren't able to work or earn an income for a short period of time.

2. Not all debt is bad. When you distinguish between credit used to fund the purchase of something that will increase your wealth and debt created for disposable items, you are empowering yourself to make informed financial decisions.

Why is referring to credit use "bad" keeping you locked in debt? Judgments like this will translate back to yourself and you will end up feeling like you are a bad person with no discipline or self-control. This sort of language and self-talk will end up creating a self-fulfilling prophecy – unless you can learn to turn your view around and use the debt as an opportunity to reflect on past expenditures you have made. Things to consider are: Why was the expenditure made? How much was spent? Over what time period were the expenditures made? What can you do about it? And, at the same time, always show gratitude for all the enjoyment you have received from the items and experiences that were purchased on credit and have created the debt. Look for ways to turn the debt into credit that will increase your financial position.

3. A judgment that says that consumer debt is bad will not inspire change or motivate you to reduce it. While this is certainly the desired outcome, very few people are motivated to move away from something. We are all far more motivated to move towards something that inspires us. When looking at your debt, such as your credit card debt or consolidated loans, these can provide valuable clues about the income of your desired lifestyle.

How? By totaling your consumer debt and dividing it by the approximate number of months you took to accumulate it, you will have a number that represents the cost of your real lifestyle.

You then have three choices: increase your income by that amount plus some extra, decrease your expenses by that amount or a combination of both.

4. To reduce and eliminate consumer debt, you have to think in terms of multiples of threes: Plan to earn three times as much money as you have been over-spending by; plan to reduce your expenses by three times the amount you have been over-spending by; or plan to have it take three times as long to eliminate the debt as it took to accumulate it. If this seems like a daunting, impossible task, then you need some new strategies, because when you try to sacrifice for too long, you will eventually set yourself up for failure.

   How do you move beyond the debt? You need to set a goal, discover the reason for moving beyond and what the rewards along the way will be.

5. A consolidation of consumer debt, while often easy and certainly accessible, should always be the last resort if you are carrying consumer debt; a loan gets carried for longer, the original purpose gets lost and the awareness and habits that support long-term wealth are not considered. An organized debt elimination strategy is far more effective and less expensive. If a consolidation does become necessary, the first strategy would be to consider only some of the outstanding loans, combined with a planned elimination strategy, rather than for all of the outstanding loans together.

   Why? Because, for heaven's sake, a debt elimination strategy is just that. It is not a way to reduce interest charges or a way to enable savings at the same time. It is a debt elimination strategy, period! It is the best investment you can make if it has gotten to the point of being difficult to manage and mostly consisting of lifestyle and/or consumer expenses. Don't try to justify it as anything else.

MoneyMinding I CAN Stories for Step 9:

Susan's story: "I have been at home with my kids since they were born. Except for the little bit of music I play professionally, I haven't worked outside the home for over ten years. My husband is a retired consultant who now loves investing. I wanted something else to do and have considered several business ideas around decorating and home design, but nothing seemed to really inspire me. When I heard that my favorite retail store was for sale, I couldn't believe it. I couldn't sleep. I couldn't stop thinking about it. I tracked down the owner to get the details and was ready to buy the store right then and there. Until, we looked at the details. That's when I realized I knew nothing about buying a business; very little about leasing, independent retailing, insurance, inventory valuation, debit and credit card issues and all the other business aspects. I knew marketing and I knew the product – that was it.

What had to happen was a serious review of the numbers and legal aspects, as well as a check-in with my family and life priorities to balance out the emotional excitement of the moment. I guess I really needed to have a whole life plan, not just a business to buy. In a very short time, I started asking questions and was introduced to people who were experts on all these areas I knew nothing about. I even created a business plan before submitting my offer to purchase. Without the whole step-by-step approach of asking a lot of people a lot of questions, I would have made an emotional decision that wasn't supported with a solid plan to build and run a profitable business. I would have acted on the excitement of the moment rather than considering my family priorities. Instead, I was able to use the emotional excitement to ask a lot of questions; do a lot of research and create a wonderful plan to balance my home and work life in a way that supports all my needs and have a profitable, fun business at the same time."

Simple Step 10:
Incoming Producing Assets

Invest in assets to produce income (real estate, businesses, income stocks).

Prosperity Principle:

Learn and implement financial savvy. There are universal strategies for saving, investing, giving and spending money as well as the specific tax, investment and insurance rules that apply to your individual circumstance. Both the principles and the rules can be learned and implemented easily if you know where to turn for advice and what specific results you're looking for.

Significant Strategy:

If you learn to practice delayed gratification and to pay cash for all luxury items, then you always know if you can afford something before buying it. This will eliminate debt. Debt, created from the accumulation of liabilities, will control you and is the biggest obstacle to financial independence.

Miracle Money Multipliers for Step 10:

1. What is your exit plan? Before you invest, you need to decide when and how you will get out. When you borrow, it's the same thing: how and when can you pay this back? When you purchase something, how long will you have it and when and how will you dispose of it?

When do you establish the exit plan? Every single financial transaction to spend, borrow, invest or insure starts with the end in mind. This means that before you sign an agreement to purchase, you also know when and how you will sell, close or exit the program. If you haven't done this yet, then do it now. What are your overall financial goals? What are your priorities? Given the programs you have in place, when and how will you sell them or eliminate them from your financial life?

2. To focus on accumulating a large sum of money that you can withdraw at a later date will create stress. A more effective and empowering focus is to consider the purpose of the accumulated funds. For example, if you are working to set aside a sum of money (say $1 million) to support yourself when you leave work (i.e. when you retire), this number is not a number most people relate to. If you, instead, focus on creating $5,000 per month so you can leave work, it's a more relatable, everyday number.

   How do you figure out what this number is? Start with your ideal budget for your ideal lifestyle then work backwards from that figure. Stay focused on that monthly income number rather than the bigger, off-in-the-distance number that doesn't relate to day-to-day financial activities.

3. Are you focused on your net worth or your income and expenses? If you are focused on income-producing assets, your net worth will take care of itself if you also keep an eye on expenses. Your plan is to develop assets that provide income; to leverage any debt to increase your income; to maintain control over your expenses so you can build these income-producing assets. Your plan is not to build a net worth that needs to be supported by your income. Your plan is not to focus on the difference between your income and expenses. Your plan is to build a net worth that produces ongoing income.

86

Why? Increasing your income will increase your net worth, which will increase your income, which will increase your net worth, etc. Income and net worth are connected and if you miss this connection, there will be a "disconnect" between current spending and overall financial well-being and between accumulated assets, net worth and day-to-day living.

4. How do you know where to start with investing? Well, besides having the proper foundation, time, space and support, it is important to begin to develop your own strategies. You can learn from others by emulating them, studying them and adapt their style to your own, but because we all have different interests, reference points and access to information at different times, one of the first ways to begin to develop your own personal investment strategy to do an evaluation of your interests. Do some research and start to notice what companies, what aspects of companies, what type of investments and how the information is presented to you that makes you take notice.

When do you start this process? Now. Even if you don't have an investment portfolio and you don't have money to invest, you can read the newspaper and watch the business news. You can pay attention to trends, activities of stores or businesses that you know about and are interested in. Start to cultivate a financial interest in the things you are already interested in – write down headlines, types of businesses and company names. Then, start asking questions about potential investment opportunities or moneymaking ideas.

A MoneyMinding I CAN Story for Step 10:

Teresa's story: "All my life I've either had money, or not. There never seemed to be a middle ground. Unfortunately, my husband died at a point in our life where we had very little. Originally, I wanted to learn how to make more money on the investments I had. I thought that with

some effort on my part, I could earn over fifteen percent consistently and be able to grow my meager investment account to something significant that would support me in a pretty good lifestyle. I was starting with about $50,000 and I wanted to have $500,000!

I'm single and approaching 60. I implemented some creative financial savvy to enable me to learn and to interact with my money on a regular basis. It actually made the process of learning about investing quite simple and understandable. Unfortunately, my plan called for me to start with a base of income generating investments, which created my first obstacle. My portfolio was either too small for most advisors or they would look at it and tell me I might want to have more realistic goals.At one point, I got so frustrated that when my sister told me about an off-shore investment she was involved in and making 35% on each transaction, I abandoned my entire plan and thought I could get in and out quickly then start over with the plan. Well, I got in fast enough, and out too. Only thing was I got out because the whole thing ended up being a scam and I got out with no money. At least none of what I invested.

I did finally go back to my plan, but this time I focused on earning income to support the assets, which would produce more income, which would increase my investments, and on and on. My money is now invested, but in more moderate earning companies and I'm active in selecting the investments for some of the money invested to help me learn and develop my skills before going into higher risk investments again.

At the same time, I'm almost finished writing a book with a friend. We are developing a business strategy around licensing and selling products related to the book content on the Internet. Its interesting how what originally seemed to be the slow path to wealth, is likely going to turn into the fast path because we're having fun, we're making money and we'll even be able to positively make a difference in other peoples' lives when the book and business are complete.

I have also increased my goal to $750,000 with even more conviction to know that it will happen!"

Simple Step 11:
Growth Assets

Establish investments for long-term growth and financial independence.

Prosperity Principle:

Eliminate self-defeating language and be aware of the words you use everyday that prevent you from achieving success. "Can't", "should", "try" and "hope" are easy to recognize and easy to change. This simple shift in language will have a profound impact on your overall attitude because, "What you say is what you hear, and what you hear is what you believe." If your mouth is constantly speaking negatively, your mind will also think negatively. Rather than saying "don't forget," say "remember" instead and you'll be happy you did.

Significant Strategy:

Measure your progress daily. You will need to devise systems for tracking and measuring your results. You will be able to see success unfold and learn where to concentrate more effort by recording your journey.

Miracle Money Multipliers for Step 11:

1. Risk means different things to different people. We most commonly refer to it as the probability of loss. It is important to know ahead of time what your ability to withstand loss is. For example, no one is going to realistically invest money with the

probability of losing everything. Instead, they will invest with a percentage of assets they feel comfortable risking.

How do you know how much to risk? If $10,000 was invested, you might decide you could reasonably withstand a $1,000 loss; therefore, you would have a ten percent risk. This then becomes the foundation of your exit plan. If you are close to losing ten percent of your money, then you have already decided this is the point when you leave that particular investment. This concept is the same for investments that increase in price as well. If you have a nice gain on paper, then you simply apply the same percentage to the price increase. If your original $10,000 investment increases to $20,000, then your new amount of money at risk would likely be $2,000 or ten percent of the new price, unless you decide to completely withdraw your original investment, and apply the same original 10% factor to the money that stays invested.

Other factors to consider are the overall value of an investment relative to your total investments, and whether you have already recaptured your original investment capital in a previous transaction. The concept is that you establish the exit parameters ahead of time and you pre-determine how much of an investment is at risk at any given time.

2. Under no circumstances would you plan to make an investment where there could be a potential 100% loss which would devastate your life. For this reason, you need to have an insurance plan, loss protection strategy and exit plan in place for every investment. It is not prudent to assume that because historically something has increased in value over the long-term that history will repeat it self. Always make a personal decision and implement a plan for when, how and why you will sell your investment.

Why? While there are no guarantees, if your only plan is to hold for the long-term, you are sure to either lose money or lose sleep at some point during the life of the investment. When you decide how much you can comfortably risk losing, you maintain control over the process and confidence in your overall financial situation.

A MoneyMinding I CAN Story for Step 11:

Victor's story: "I am a single male in my late 40s and found myself rebuilding my life after losing everything in a business partnership gone bad. Rather than choosing bankruptcy and its consequences, I chose to dig myself out of this incredibly big hole! What I found in the process was the missing link in making money decisions – creating wealth with the emphasis on life goals, desires and priorities! I discovered I did not have to put my life on hold while building wealth! I could have BOTH at the same time – lifestyle and building wealth! It was a matter of setting goals and laying out a plan to reach those goals as laid out in MoneyMinding.

My first decision was to get out of the rental accommodation I was in and into a place of my own. That immediately cut my accommodation costs in half and created a positive cash flow that was used to eliminate all "bad" debt. My timing with the rising real estate market was ideal and in a few years the increased equity allowed me to move into a larger, very comfortable accommodation AND do some investing.

Initially, I started investing in the stock market with the help of a broker. However, that broker moved out of town and I was left on my own. I chose to learn investing on my own and gradually became more confident in my ability to make my own investment decisions. I became more and more interested in the selection process and gradually moved towards doing my own research for stock and mutual fund selection using key strategies in MoneyMinding.

I am now enjoying developing those strategies for stock market and real estate investing, all while taking wonderful holidays, spending time with family and continuing to work at my full-time job."

Simple Step 12:
Creative, Higher Risk Investments

Diversify with more short-term or more volatile investments.

Prosperity Principle:

Financial independence isn't something that happens overnight. It is a constant and progressive journey. Having more money isn't the answer to financial independence. Yet, if you don't learn this principle and other basic laws of financial success today, regardless of whether you have a significant amount of money or a small amount, where you end up tomorrow will not likely be much different from where you're starting. It is the small changes implemented consistently that will produce the massive changes over time.

Significant Strategy:

Enjoy the moment and everything that you do. Money is simply an instrument to provide you with choices. Financial independence is a journey, not a dollar amount. The process of achieving and maintaining financial independence is life-long. In order to experience true prosperity and a life of fulfillment, you need to relax, have fun and be grateful for each day and all that it provides you.

Miracle Money Multipliers for Step 12:

1. If something seems too good to be true, it could be, or it could not be. You need to find out for yourself by taking extra care, applying

extra precaution, digging deeper and maintaining appropriate control. Under no circumstance is it ever appropriate or prudent to risk your entire net worth on any investment unless you also plan to live with any resulting negative outcome.

Why? Just because you don't understand something does not necessarily make it bad. Just because your neighbor, group of associates or other person you respect has invested or participated in a particular financial strategy does not mean it is okay for you. The worst thing you can tell yourself is, "If it's okay for so and so, then it must be good for me too." Have the confidence to make your own decisions and ask your own questions. Someone else is not going to pay your bills or look after your household if something goes sideways. It's your responsibility!

2. There are different ways of earning money from investments besides buying low and selling high. In fact, an investment that produces immediate income rather than increasing in value is an example of looking sideways at the market. An investment that makes money in a dropping market is an example of buying high and selling low to make money.

Where could you find out more? You don't have to jump into every opportunity you hear about. In fact, you don't have to invest in any of them, but you can start to ask different advisors from different backgrounds in different industries about possibilities for alternative or creative investing. For example, securities options, futures, commodities, foreign exchange, derivatives, initial public offerings, private companies, etc. are all more creative investments. There are different types of returns and different types of risks. When you have a proper financial foundation, including knowledge and skills, these types of investments can be appropriate. Without a proper foundation, they might look attractive and sound appealing and, to some people, these are low risk investments. When everything else is in place – have fun

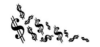

– there is great diversity and wonderful opportunities to make great returns and make a difference while you're at it – and new opportunities will come your way every day!! Yes, every day. You do not need to jump on the first one because you think it's the "chance of a lifetime." This line of thinking comes out of fear, and scarcity thinking – never a good thing.

3. The biggest risk in the financial world is lack of knowledge. What is risky to some people is boring to others. Just because someone describes something as risky (or safe, for that matter) doesn't mean you can take that at face value. Safe and risky are subjective terms that need personal evaluation based on goals, situation, timeframe, reference point, knowledge, experience, etc. A second mortgage investment or a covered call option might be the best strategy for someone's portfolio and might be considered conservative, safe investments given the right situations. However, what does the rest of the picture look like and what other influences need to be considered before making that sort of decision?

How do you know? Always start your questions with yourself. What do you know about the transaction? Why do you want it? What are your expectations? What is influencing your decision? What do you need to know? And, how and when will you get out?

A MoneyMinding I CAN Story for Step 12:

Wendy's story: "I began to be interested in financial independence and wealth building while still married. When my husband left a year ago, I put all my attention into really taking the goals that had been crystallizing within me and looking for ways to turn them into reality. I have always considered myself to be conservative and responsible with money. I find it interesting that the sort of investments and business ventures that I considered too risky or complicated a short while ago, now interest me. I guess the process is just that, a process. I find the variety of investment options available amazing. While I would have been totally

overwhelmed by the thought of even looking at some of the material just a year or so ago, I'm now browsing offering memorandums, documents for private companies and interesting investment strategies for tax deferral.

Who would have thought... I'm investing creatively; building a couple of businesses, one online and one off; and participating in a real estate investment club looking for opportunities to expand and diversify my income there too. I guess, through the system, I just finally read enough books and met enough successful people that I could finally believe it might actually be possible for even me, a single women in my 60s to make it happen. Somewhere along the line, I realized I was interested in wealth, not just for the money, but because it lets me do so much for myself and other things I believe in."

Your Next Step

Here's the really big AHA from all these steps, strategies, principles, miracle multipliers and stories: you never actually graduate from Step 12; you simply keep moving. You will be constantly revising your goals, reviewing your situation and making new decisions in light of new situations, opportunities and information.

So, here's how you're going to end these *12 Simple Steps of MoneyMinding*: you're not!!

You're going to do one, or all, of a few things:

- Reread it, but this time with a highlighter, notebook and pen so you are clearly marking the important steps, ideas and strategies to be implemented into your life today;

- Stay plugged in with the MoneyMinding FREE Fast Action Tips delivered online from www.moneyminding.com;

- Become a MoneyMinding member to help you move further along with more detailed and personal strategies.

Regardless of where you are today, that's where you start – every single day. The *12 Simple Steps of MoneyMinding* are revolving and the past is gone and the future hasn't arrived yet. So while you're revisiting your steps and implementing MoneyMinding Miracle Money Multipliers into your own life to create your very own personal success story, always remember the following important concepts to help guide your decisions:

- Believe in financial possibilities, not sacrifice.

- You can learn wealth-thinking, even if you were raised with a poverty mentality.

- It's about life, not money.

- Financial independence is measured horizontally by income, not vertically by assets alone, although the two are connected.

- Every investment decision must be simultaneously made with a loss protection plan in place.

- Fees and annual rate of return are not the most important investment selection criteria.

- Remember the value of professional advice and assistance in making financial decisions. Financial professionals will be trained and licensed and whomever you receive advice from must share your values and understand your true goals and priorities.

- Daily habits and small decisions can make a big difference positively, or negatively, in where you end up financially.

- Principles taught over 2,000 years ago in scripture about financial management are as important and relevant today as they have ever been in the past.

- People have unique desires for their life and that each person is, therefore, responsible for translating these desires into their own written goals.

- A giving attitude begins at any economic level and is not something you do when you have "achieved" or when you "feel" like it.

- There is a process and system that, when strategically implemented, will provide a foundation of good habits, education and solid solutions for you to realize your personal goals.

- Finance needs to be part of the educational curriculum for young people, beginning with primary ages, to provide training on value, small details and some simple "how to" concepts.

While you might not agree or understand all of these concepts, it is important to recognize your reaction to them and to be open-minded about what they can mean to you in your life today.

And as you move forward, here is a simple summary of some key MoneyMinding messages for you to refer to quickly and easily:

- Choose your lifestyle first, then the financial vehicles.

- Where are you going? What are you committed to? What are your real life priorities?

- It's about financial independence, not retirement.

- Financial success is horizontal continuation of income – not just vertical growth of a pool of money because we live on monthly income and day-to-day transactions – large sums are not tangible.

- Don't try, do.

- Can, not can't.

- Will, not should.

- There is a hierarchical process to assist in making effective, supportive financial decisions.

- Multiple streams of income are an integral component to financial success. For example:
  - ~ Business – network marketing, franchise, corporation
  - ~ Insurance
  - ~ Investments
  - ~ Pensions – personal, government, corporate
  - ~ Real estate – home equity, rental
  - ~ Royalties – licensing and selling
  - ~ Referrals

- We can learn to develop supportive financial habits. For example, when money comes in, the first transactions documented are for self and for giving, even if those funds are later needed for monthly commitments.

- Goals must be in writing and be personal and emotional. The money for your goals will be the result of following and achieving your true passion.

- We all have non-financial assets and resources that we can learn how to capitalize on.

- Every financial decision needs to include an exit strategy.

- Most losses can be controlled when emotional decision-making is reduced.

- Future tax implications need to be considered in all planning regardless of current financial circumstances. For example, are assets jointly held, where are they to be held, retirement savings plan premise, source of funds, deductions and credits? These are issues that can be more important than the advertised rate of return on your money.

- We receive advice from many sources – media, friends, neighbors and relatives, past experience, school and advisors; and therefore, we need to become aware of our own values and also the values of those people offering the information (their background).

- First, know yourself, then know your advisor, and finally, know your investment or financial product.

- You build your financial plan from where you are, beginning with a base, then developing confidence and habits to expand.

- Always get professional advice from people who understand your goals and share your values.

- Always know your expectations for a transaction and know why and what the potential consequences of failure might be.

I'm looking forward to hearing your MoneyMinding I CAN success story!! Remember, it's improvement that's constant and never-ending – have fun and enjoy the process!!

Abundant blessings
to you always,

Tracy

About Tracy Piercy

Tracy Piercy is a Certified Financial Planner who has learned in her 16 years in the financial services industry that money is so much more than the numbers. She has studied with some of the greatest success teachers today: Tony Robbins, Robert Allen, Mark Victor Hansen, Robert Kiyosaki, Michael Gerber, Harv Ecker; she has read over 400 books on financial success; teaches advisors; consults to the industry on the psychology of money; in addition to having been a successful investment and insurance advisor herself.

The *12 Simple Steps of MoneyMinding®* evolved from her own struggle and recovery from a major financial loss immediately followed by a death, cancer and divorce in her family. "I just wanted my life back, and needed something to take us one small step at a time. I got that, and so much more. It has worked for me; for thousands of others and I believe it will work for you too."

Tracy donates a percentage of all her earnings to charitable causes through the MoneyMinding Foundation formed to support financial literacy and empowerment programs. She has a wonderful husband of 11-plus years, and together they live in scenic Victoria, British Columbia, Canada with their beautiful daughter and small dog. They live in a century-old home, surrounded by great friends and family.